REDISCOVERING F

REDISCOVERING FREEDOM

JOHN LESTER

AND

PIERRE SPOERRI

GROSVENOR

LONDON · MELBOURNE
OTTAWA · SALEM OREGON · WELLINGTON

First published 1992
GROSVENOR BOOKS
54 Lyford Road
London SW18 3JJ

251 Bank Street
Ottawa, Ontario K2P 1X3

21 Dorcas Street
South Melbourne
Victoria 3205, Australia

PO Box 1834, Wellington
New Zealand

GROSVENOR USA
3735 Cherry Avenue NE
Salem, Oregon 97303
USA

Designed by Blair Cummock
Cover Design by Dell Williams
Cover picture: detail from a painting by Olly and Suzi,
6ft by 5ft, acrylic and oil stick on canvas
Back cover photographs by David Channer

British Library Cataloguing-in-publication Data:
A catalogue record of this book is available
from the British Library

ISBN 1-85239-016-6

Photoset in Sabon by Derek Doyle and Associates, Mold
Printed and bound by Biddles Ltd, Guildford, England

Acknowledgments

We would like to express our gratitude to all those who have helped us with this book. Among them, Christine Karrer, Angela Willoughby, Elizabeth Lester and Daphne Waterston who typed the original drafts, Bill Stallybrass who searched for the official English translations of the French and German texts which we have quoted, and Michael Hutchinson who helped prepare all the footnotes. Our special thanks go to Ailsa Hamilton without whose editing skills and detailed care this book might well not have seen the light of day.

Contents

Foreword
A Central European Perspective

In this book you are a guest.

You are being invited to take part
in an intriguing and sincere conversation
with two friends, Pierre Spoerri and John Lester.

The conversation has no predetermined objectives.
It is open-ended.
But it is being conducted under one underlying and vital
condition:
it has to be completely honest.
Its subject is freedom.

Many-faceted, wide-ranging exploration
of its meanings, its applications
– and misapplications.
Really – how free is freedom?

But soon, very soon,
one is discovering that in parallel and less explicitly
another basic concept, another experience is being explored
– an experience of honesty.

Their interdependence is vital and dynamic:
with every turn of conversation,
with every chapter,
as the meaning of freedom becomes clearer,
and as the experience of inner freedom perceived
is expanded and more firmly established,
honesty is similarly deepened and grows to become more and
more inclusive.
And it is a very demanding mistress.

Eventually it claims the whole of life – and liberates it.
The more areas of life are submitted to it
– the greater are the rewards.
But it would be foolish – and dishonest –
to claim that it is an easy task.

The great attraction of this book and the pleasure of its
conversation is that one is taken through so many layers of
freedom – and of enslavement, of unfreedom, by two very
gentle people. They go along unhurriedly, at our pace. And
they offer not only their intellectual discipline and wide
experience of life, but their friendship as well. So as one
travels along with them one is increasingly invited to take
part in their conversations, to be a co-author of the book.
And in our own inner dialogue we are also challenged to
become clearer about our values, freer in our thinking and
decision-making, more honest with ourselves. Hard stuff –
but so gently offered, and with such humility.

What authority have they, Pierre and John, to take us on?
To be so personal by being so open? How wide, how
authentic is their life experience? And on what grounds have
I, writing this introduction, to invite you to this intimate
conversation, to commend their book so wholeheartedly to
you?

Pierre grew up in a very special atmosphere of university
life in Zurich, where his father was Vice-Chancellor. He
studied himself at the universities of Geneva and Zurich.
Early in his life he became, with his father, involved in Moral
Re-Armament. He travelled very widely, meeting a great
number of people, participating as an honest broker in many
delicate negotiations, going to some of the more complex
regions of Africa and Asia wherever he saw a glimmer of hope
of reconciliation and greater inner freedom and peace flowing
from it. As a journalist he has access to places often closed to
most people. In a quiet way he is successful in this field.

He establishes excellent contacts with younger people,
listening to them very attentively as he discerns prophetic
voices in their longings.

Married to Fulvia who comes from landowning German
gentry of pre-1940 Latvia, he has learned about the different

attitudes of country people. And of those who after centuries of settled life lost every possession and just escaped with their lives. For an essentially urban person from such a peaceful and stable haven as Switzerland all this is a mind-opening experience.

John comes from the busy English Midlands. As a doctor he meets people at their most vulnerable. He is married to Elizabeth, daughter of Dr and Mrs Kenneth McAll, who have spent many years as missionaries and doctors in China. Kenneth has written a widely known and significant book, *Healing the Family Tree*.

John, as well as Pierre, has travelled extensively in order to meet people and has stayed several years in India. They have two sons who are still studying.

John is now the Secretary of Moral Re-Armament in Britain, responsible for a great deal of organising of meetings and publications. As well as all this he also practises as a doctor in West London.

The work that Pierre and John do (and Fulvia and Elizabeth with them) does not fill a convenient box. They are involved in so many things not because they are ambitious – just the reverse – but because they feel that God, to whom they listen attentively every morning, prompts them to be responsive to the needs of our times and responsible for more than just their own lives. Yes, they are God-centred people willing to be vulnerable, deeply committed.

And what about myself? I come from Poland. I lost everything, including my father in a Soviet prison, during World War II and was deported to Siberia in 1940. In 1942, by a not far from miraculous quirk of fate, what remained of the family was allowed to leave the Soviet Union. Since that time we have lived for eight years in the Middle East and then in the freedom of the West. In gratitude for this deliverance and greatly helped by my wife Aniela and our four children, I am deeply involved in Polish and European affairs and in the Catholic Church. Through this work we have met Pierre and John and MRA. For this rare privilege, which was really a life-changing experience, we are deeply grateful.

From this perspective and commitment it is clear that the issues raised in this book are most relevant and of vital importance for our times, and especially for the recovery of human values and rebuilding of civilised societies in Central and Eastern Europe.

Ultimately the success or failure of the experiment of building a European Community, of the renovation of European civilisation after the scourge of Communism and Nazism, and indeed the fate of Europe as a whole, depends on our deeper understanding and commitment to real freedom.

A listening ear and heart, humility, honesty and commitment are the ways to take on this task. Immensely important, wonderfully liberating, full of promise. John and Pierre, Pierre and John – we thank you.

Olgierd Michal Stepan

Vice-President, Pastoral Council for Polish Communities in
Western Europe
Member of Administrative Council of John Paul II Foundation

Introduction

HOW DID WE, an English doctor and a Swiss journalist, come to tackle such a major subject as freedom, and choose to do it together? Both of us, in the course of our work, have travelled to many parts of the world, including countries which were then under Communist rule.

We saw behind the so-called Iron Curtain that particular, uniform, greyness that belongs to totalitarian regimes. We saw the almost total limitation of individual freedom, which had been present for decades. Yet in the homes of many of those we met we found colour, diversity, hope and humour. Among some we found a remarkable inner liberty, not always matched in the West.

In our own countries we had both observed that though everyone had almost unlimited freedom, there were plenty of people who remained imprisoned – within themselves. Whilst the environment was full of colour and diversity, it was possible to see in the lives of some a sad conformity.

This paradox, we felt, required further study and thought. Conversations with many people, representing all kinds of views, faiths and nationalities, both broadened and deepened our thinking and made us want to share with others the insights we had been given. Our own perspectives spring from our Christian faith and our Western European background. The more intellectual approach of the 'continental' and the pragmatic Anglo-Saxon one turned out to be an asset rather than a problem.

Freedom is, after all, on most people's agenda. The demise of hated totalitarian regimes, principally in Eastern and Central Europe, overjoyed a world which had come to regard them as permanent. Their collapse revealed the barrenness of the ideas behind them, the empty shops told their own story. The lies and cruelty endured by so many became public knowledge.

Many who were for so long unable to communicate

13

normally with the rest of the world, turned to the West for help – material help certainly, but also the free exchange of ideas and values. Yet, as this happened the West also was revealed in its barrenness as well as its plenty.

Western inadequacy, for example, was shown up when the collapse of Communism left the way open for a surge of old nationalistic forces, which had been considered dead and buried by many of the most knowledgeable observers. It is not enough to deplore the excessive nationalism which can only achieve its aims at the cost of other nations and of its own minorities. Our record in the West on nationalism has not been good either. It has become obvious that Western political ideas and institutions cannot by themselves fill the vacuum left behind by a decayed ideology. There is a new dimension of thought and life needed.

For us in the West it is hard to grasp what life would be like without freedom. People only become conscious of it when they are losing it or have lost it. How do we transmit freedom's values to a generation that takes it for granted and has never had to defend it?

As we examined the inner liberty possessed by our friends in Eastern Europe, we discovered that it often sprang from deeply held spiritual values. As the East has turned to the West what has it found? Our freedom of initiative and of communication, our open society, our free markets point the way to material prosperity. Is that prosperity possible without the acceptance at the same time of indulgent values, which shrink the human spirit? These have arisen in the West, we would suggest, not from freedom itself but from a secular interpretation of it, and the loss of faith which that interpretation has encouraged.

Religious faith, marginalised in the West and previously persecuted or proscribed in the East, far from limiting freedom, may yet hold the key to real inner liberty, the most precious of the freedoms we seek.

Eastern Europe may have clarified the issue of freedom, but in other parts of the world the struggle continues. There are still many people crying out for freedom. The future of human society may depend on the interplay of two questions: Can people who are denied freedom by the state remain in captivity for ever? And can those who misuse freedom retain it for ever? The first question is being answered by events. The second is more difficult, but is relevant for us all.

We may all need to review our values. Just as religion, which had been held down for so long, played a constructive role in helping to end the tyranny of Communism in Eastern Europe, so we in the West may also need to look at our spiritual heritage: the margin of society may not be its rightful place. When it comes to the proper use of the freedoms we have gained, we have as much to learn as to give.

The book that has emerged from our conversations concentrates particularly on inner freedom, within the context of society and its desire for external liberty; for we believe that the two are linked. How do we revitalise the deepest aspects of our humanity, break the fears that keep us wedded to accepted paths and norms, and allow our sense of inner adventure to grow? What are the deepest motivations that are available? Is there something stronger than ambition, bitterness or the desire for prosperity?

Its setting is philosophical, but not in an academic sense. Edmund Burke wrote at the time of the American Revolution: 'Men are fitted for civic freedom in exact proportion to their readiness to put moral chains on their own appetites. Society cannot exist if there are no in-built brakes somewhere to its uncontrolled will and appetite, and the fewer of these exist inside man himself, the more they have to be applied from outside. It is part of the external law that men of uncontrolled character cannot be free. Their passions create for them their own chains.'

Most people, when they are being honest, know that many of the real difficulties which they face are human, moral dilemmas. 'Their own chains' all too often remain hidden; some even imagine they are the only ones with such difficulties. In the setting of the world we all like to reveal a confident face. In the setting of the doctor's surgery it is clear that many of us privately long for help. For these reasons, therefore, we have taken the liberty of quoting from the personal experiences of individuals and in many cases from our own. If inner liberty is something we want, and realise we do not possess, the search for it will need to be at a deep enough level.

1 Freedom in Captivity and Dictatorship

John Lester and Pierre Spoerri

IN THE SEVENTIES and eighties the countries of the Communist world, which had maintained central power by an almost total control of their peoples, found that they were falling further and further behind their Western counterparts in their standard of living. The Soviet Union came more and more to resemble a Third World country, in spite of its importance on the international stage.

A great dilemma for these nations was that modern technology provides an ease of communication, freedom of information and flexibility which were not compatible with their system. Without it they could not compete with the rest of the world; with it they could not continue the tight central control which required secrecy. Further, societies that have been closed for years, built on austerity and strict discipline of their populations, are particularly vulnerable when they open themselves to the world. A Chinese diplomat asked us one year before the massacre on Tiananmen Square brought to an end their steps towards greater openness, 'How can we open our society more to the rest of the world without our people becoming more selfish?' A student from the same country added, 'Is it possible for us to have Western technological excellence without having Western moral decadence?'

During these years, anyone in the West interested in the future of these countries was faced with many fundamental and practical obstacles. It was possible to visit friends in Eastern Europe, for example, as a tourist. But those who had any connection – as we had – with groups who believed in the primary importance of faith and freedom, had to expect that the people they met would be faced with increased scrutiny, and sometimes persecution, from the authorities.

Two other ways were open to those who wanted to

understand what was really happening in those countries. The literature coming out of the East – officially and unofficially – allowed some insights into what people were thinking and how they were living 'behind the Curtain'. And for many of us opportunities were offered to meet some of those who had voluntarily or involuntarily left their fatherland to live in the West. It was an unforgettable experience, for example, to meet, in the sixties, two of the personalities described by Alexander Solzhenitsyn in *The First Circle* and to hear their experiences directly.

Another outstanding personality to catch the eye of the world during these decades was the Czech President Václav Havel. His *Letters to Olga*[1] – a record of the weekly letters sent in the course of six years' imprisonment to his wife – are one of the great human documents of this period.

Then and later Havel did a lot of thinking about freedom. During one of his visits to Western Europe after the liberation of his country, he was asked what it was like suddenly to find himself President. 'He replied that everyone kept coming up to him asking what they should do with their freedom. This inability to trust themselves, this fear of responsibility, he said, was one of the scars that 45 years of Communism had inflicted on the psyche of a once-free people. The Czechs and Slovaks had passed through a very dark tunnel at the end of which there was a light of freedom. Unexpectedly they had passed through prison gates and had found themselves in a square. They were now free and they did not know where to go.'[2]

Havel is just one of a group who may be able to teach us a great deal about freedom – the men and women who suffered in prison and detention camps for many years of their lives. A fresh look at what freedom means may well be offered by some of these men and women, who paid a high price to preserve their faith and dignity.

It is hardly surprising that people who have survived the hell of the Gulag do not mince words when they talk about the hypocrisy of some aspects of Western life. Vladimir Bukovsky says: 'I think that many people in the Western countries have forgotten what freedom and democracy really are. To them they have become part of a comfortable and undemanding way of life, to achieve a high standard of living, to have a good time. But I am afraid that many forget that democracy and freedom are above all the right to fight. Remember that your freedom ends at that very point where your solidarity with the persecuted ends.'[3]

The Polish Nobel Prize winner Czeslaw Milosz wrote the unforgettable words on the monument of the three crosses in memory of those who died in Gdansk in December 1970.*

Milosz asked in an earlier essay *The Captive Mind*: 'What goes on in the heads of the Western masses? Isn't Christianity dying out in the West, and aren't its people bereft of all faith? Isn't there a void in their heads? Don't they fill that void with chauvinism, detective stories, and artistically worthless movies? Well then, what can the West offer us? Freedom from something is a great deal, yet not enough. It is much less than freedom for something.'[4]

Some of the dissident writers go even further by analysing in depth what has happened to them since they left the 'unfree' for the 'free' world. The Czech writer Pavel Kohout says, 'I do not consider myself to be freer here in the West than I was in Czechoslovakia (during the Communist time), because I was a free man there too. I was only unfree where external conditions were concerned... There I was an object to be manipulated; but within this attempted manipulation I preserved for myself an absurd inner freedom. Here I have to fight for it, as it is so similar to external freedom, while not being the same.'[5]

    * You, who wronged a simple man,
      Bursting into laughter at the crime,
      And kept a crowd of fools around you,
      Mixing good and evil to blur the line,
      Though everyone bowed down before you,
      Saying Virtue and Wisdom lit your way,
      Striking gold medals in your honour,
      – And glad to have survived another day,
      Do not feel safe. The poet remembers.
      You can slay him, but another is always born ...
      The words are written down, the deed, the date.
      You would have done better with a winter's dawn,
      A rope, and a branch bent down beneath your weight.[6]

The Russian human rights activist Natan Sharansky writes, 'The most important thing is to hear the free soul within ourselves. But you see, people don't often let themselves hear their soul freely. It was this sense of inner freedom that I found in the prisons of the Soviet Union which kept me alive and which will help keep me alive.'[7]

Even more important than this comparison between East and West is what these people, through the experience of the prison camps, have discovered about the nature of man himself. When a person has reached the point of losing everything, even life itself, real values come to the surface: the point of decision is reached.

The psychiatrist Viktor Frankl was incarcerated for several years in a concentration camp. He asked himself whether an inmate of such a camp has to submit to the conditions, whether there comes a moment when 'he cannot do anything else'. He writes, 'Well, we can answer this question both on the basis of conviction and experience, as life in the camps has shown us that human beings "can live differently" ... that there is a remnant of spiritual freedom, a remnant of an attitude of freedom that persists even in this situation of seemingly absolute coercion, both outward and inward... Even if those who achieved it were few, they are the proof that one can take everything from a person in a concentration camp but this last human freedom, to react to certain circumstances in one way or in another. And there was this "one way or another"... The spiritual freedom of man, which cannot be taken away from him up to the last breath of his life, allows him up to that last breath, to give meaning to his life in a creative way.'[8]

Our own experience, as we travelled and shared briefly the environment of control and coercion, was that these insights on inner freedom were borne out in the lives of many we met. Courage was widespread and tangible and should not be forgotten now that the need of it is not so obvious. In many the tyranny of fear had been broken. It is surely unlikely that political freedom would have resurfaced had this not been so.

The most personal of all the freedoms for which men and women yearn is the freedom to believe. It is our relationship with God which in the end we guard with our lives. It is that relationship above all with which no other person and no state has the right to interfere. There are millions who have no such relationship and who see no sense in such weight being given to it. There are plenty who have lost such a relationship. But those who have it cherish it above all else. History is full of men and women in every age who have accepted martyrdom rather than defile the depths of their own souls.

There is a paradox. In those parts of the world which tried deliberately to obliterate faith in God there has been a strengthening of that faith. Because it brings inner freedom even in the midst of external tyranny, it has been and ultimately always will be the instrument of external freedom also. But in those parts of the world which have for long been politically free, there has been a decline of faith which is damaging to the future of the very liberty which makes possible its loss. It would indeed be a tragedy for the world if it became the loss of faith and standards in the West which prevented the newly free countries from achieving their fullest potential.

The steps to inner freedom will be different from person to person. A Russian philosopher, Vladimir Zelinsky, described in 1989 his own journey to inner freedom: 'First came a freedom from the yoke of the state which stops you thinking your own thoughts. Then there was the discovery of God, of an inner freedom, of a world full of the unexpected, the miraculous, of divine love for each individual. Finally, I've learnt that inner freedom can't just be our private property. We must share it and refuse the privilege of being free alongside others who are not free.'[9]

In his *Underground Notes* the Yugoslav writer Mihailo Mihailov writes, 'The experiences of loss of freedom have proved that every human being is in a position to create for himself a state of complete freedom, and that it is within his power to change the world on the basis of the mystical law. Experience has further shown that the fate of men is not decided by earthly powers, by outward, physical forces, but only by the mystical power which from time immemorial has been called God and whose relationship to man seems to depend on man's relationship to his inner voice...

'No external organisation of society saves man. Nor does it liberate him. The following of the inner voice frees man, even at the gates of death. It is doubtful that there is anything more hope-giving in this world than the realisation that it is possible to influence world events in a concrete way, by heeding only the liberating voice of the soul. And no outside forces can take away this freedom. Only man himself can stop it.'[10]

2 Free to Listen

Pierre Spoerri

I READ IN a German newspaper recently, 'It takes a child two or three years to learn to talk; it takes a man a whole life-time to learn to listen.' No wonder Dr Frank Buchman,[1] whose ability to listen was extraordinary, quoted time and again, 'God gave us two ears and one mouth; why don't we listen twice as much as we talk?'[2]

The ability to be silent and to listen to the other person is a faculty rarely encountered in Western society. In school we are supposed to listen to our teachers, but what most of us learn is the art of the quick reply. And that art persists into public life. What counts is to get your point in as fast and forcefully as possible; the context is less important. Unless you sell what you have to say without hesitation or scruple, nothing will get across. That anyway seems to be the theory.

But sooner or later, the longing for silence, and perhaps too the longing to find somebody who is ready to listen, makes itself felt. By then, our own ability to express or to hear the deeper notes, or even the half-tones, in a conversation may already have been lost. But we can unlearn bad habits. The restoration of this inner balance is certainly as vital as the fulfilment of other ambitions.

I have had the privilege of visiting both Christian and Buddhist monasteries and meeting monks and nuns who have devoted their life to service in silence. I have spent unforgettable days in the Korean Buddhist monastery of Hain-Sa and in the Dalai Lama's exile monastery in Dharamsala, in the foothills of the Himalayas. In Germany, I am glad to be a friend of several Benedictine monks in the monastery of Maria Laach, near Bonn.

There is a price to pay for the true detachment, joy and freedom which are apparent in men and women dedicated to this kind of life. When a group visited the Abbess of a Cistercian convent in Switzerland, she was asked when she and the sisters had gone to the chapel for prayers that morning. She said, laughing, 'Oh, this morning we slept in. We sang the Christmas vigils from 9.30 yesterday evening until 1.30 in the morning, so we slept until 5 instead of 3.'

Nobody expects ordinary working men and women to get up at 3am to pray. But the question remains: how can any of us with normal professional and family responsibilities make enough room for silence and the inner restoration it brings? Giving adequate place to silence will not automatically solve all personal problems; but such a conscious decision may be needed to prevent our inner life from gradually drying up.

I discovered very early on from my father what a difference inner listening can make to family relationships. In the early thirties we lived in Zurich in a house not far from the university, where he was a successful university professor. Every day, when he came back from his lectures, we heard his steps going up the stairs before he disappeared into his study on the second floor. My mother reigned supreme on the ground floor, where she occupied the Ministries of Education, Justice, Interior, Food and Finance with great Swiss efficiency. She complained that she had to take all the decisions; my father, just Under-Secretary for Foreign Affairs, complained that nobody in the family realized what an important contribution he was making to the world of thought and philosophy. My bedroom was next to my parents'. I heard them argue at nights. I could not get the words but the music was unmistakable.

In 1932, a student of my father's came back from a visit to Oxford. He had the courage to tell his professor that he thought he had just found what both of them were missing. He suggested that my father should go to Geneva where a certain Frank Buchman and his international team would be holding meetings. Father was sceptical but intrigued – or desperate – enough to make the trip and to arrive at the meeting without announcing himself. He was even more intrigued by what he heard, and finally approached one of the people who had spoken from the platform. He asked how he could find the kind of freedom and joy that he had noticed in all those who had spoken. When he was told that the experiment was quite simple, that the essential elements were time, a pencil and a piece of paper, and the readiness to examine his life in the light of absolute honesty, purity, unselfishness and love,[3] he started to argue. He said that all this sounded much too simple, that he had studied philosophy for years and that he was constantly writing down his thoughts. Still, he left Geneva with the desire to try an honest experiment.

When he found himself alone in his study a few mornings later, he expected to get some very 'moral' thoughts: that he should be more patient with his wife, or that he should not let impure thoughts dominate so many of his dreams. But the thought that presented itself with great clarity was, 'Come down from your second floor!' It touched the essence of his daily life. He had succeeded in keeping aloof from all that could trouble or disturb him by disappearing into his ivory tower whenever he felt like it. For days after that first experiment, my father refused to accept the thought. Then, a second thought came: 'If God can put such a thought into your mind – and you know that it did not come from you – then to accept it or refuse it is a serious matter. You can refuse it, but you may regret it all your life.'

The day my father decided to 'come down from his second floor' the tension in our home lifted. My mother and father started to communicate with each other more effectively – especially as they also began to listen to God every morning together. And we, as children, noticed a great difference in their attitudes towards us.

That basic experiment which my father tried out in 1932 is so simple that it is available to everybody. It is universal. And yet, when such a time for listening is proposed, many of us feel some deep resistance. Why do we find it so difficult to listen? Why are we afraid of silence? In my case, it is sometimes because I already think I know, and sometimes because I hate to admit that I could be wrong. Or sometimes my mind is too full of other things. Often I need first of all to get rid of some of the 'junk' that has assembled over the last 24 hours – or even over the years. The resistance can also come from the fear of hearing something that may disturb my routine, my pleasant rhythm of life, my habits.

Then, if the experiment is to work, it entails sacrificing

time; without being ready to take enough time, life will always remain superficial. There are no hard and fast rules for this. For obvious reasons the early morning, when I am fresh and when the day needs to be planned, is a natural moment to take time to listen. The precondition is, of course, to be able to get up early enough. Pope John XXIII wrote in his *Journal of a Soul*: 'Go to bed a little earlier in the evening and arise punctually at 5.30 in the morning.' But for equally obvious reasons, many busy people find the early morning hours an impossible time for reflection and quiet. Clearly, nobody can propose the pattern for another person. But without some sacrifice, there can be no breakthrough to a new life.

Each person and each character has specific needs, specific strengths and weaknesses. One clear distinction, for instance, is between extroverts and introverts. The Chaplain of Notre Dame University, Morton Kelsey, writes, 'Since extroverts find meaning among people and in doing things, their prayer life will probably be geared to service with and to others. They are likely to find God more often present in the outer physical world than through inner experiences of quiet. Yet, extroverts also need time for quiet and reflection; otherwise they have no chance to integrate what they have experienced among others and find its significance for their own growth and their deeper relationship with God.

'Introverts, on the other hand, already find the inner world fascinating and easy to deal with. They are very likely to have no trouble finding an inner experience of God's presence, and then look down on those persons who find their meaning largely in the outer world. Their need then is to be called back to the outer world in service to other humans and to society, which is difficult but necessary for them. Unless they will get out and deal with the realities of the outer world, both beautiful and sordid, their devotional life tends to become unrealistic and detached.'[4]

The experiment of listening is available to all, to people of all faiths and no faith, to Christians, Muslims and Jews, Hindus, Buddhists and Sikhs. In each faith, there are scriptures describing the process in different religious or spiritual terms. What is common to all is that in such moments each one of us is given the chance to look at our life, our relationships and our work from a larger perspective. Uncertainties can become certitudes. Secret doubts can transform themselves into a clear 'yes' or a clear 'no'. Forgotten people or memories can reappear. Unclear thoughts can take a definite shape. And unconnected ideas can fall into place.

'One benefit of listening to God is *liberation*,' writes Klaus Bockmühl, a German theologian. 'Listening makes us independent of illegitimate human influence; it liberates us from worn-out orthodoxies and inherited prejudices, as well as from modern oppressions, circumstances, and ambitions – not to mention overwrought emotions, whether objective or subjective, collective or personal... Listening to God serves especially to liberate us from the dominant clichés of our society... Even where there is very little social oppression, we can be shackled by countless social expectations – actual or projected. Listening to God instead of to the clamouring voices of our culture can free us from myriad personal fears and anxieties.'[5]

3   What are we Afraid of?

John Lester

THE HUMAN FACE is a miracle: it conveys so much through so little. It registers uniqueness. It reveals our roots. It measures age. It expresses the gamut of human emotions – anxiety, confidence, fear, pain, resentment, happiness, desire, affection and all their degrees and variations.

As we get older, our faces record permanently the dominant struggles of the years – happy wrinkles, sour ones, frightened ones. A person's eyes reveal more than any other part of the anatomy, perhaps because the eyes are the closest we can come to the brain and nervous tissue of an individual. It is possible to see in them life or deadness, triumph or defeat, openness or deceit.

With conversation – the gift of speech – we can say something of what we feel and we can make it truthful or deceitful: we can say all or we can hide. But our faces make it harder to deceive, for they monitor constantly our emotions and passing feelings. In speech we can absorb people's thoughts but only guess at their feelings. By a caring study of their faces we can know more of their feelings.

Why is it that what we think can usually be hidden, yet what we feel is so often revealed to those who care enough to discern? Why has nature organised life that way? At a biological level, without recognisable feelings the 'chemistry' of a relationship would not happen; there would be no romance and therefore no survival of the species. We can similarly recognise aggressive intentions and therefore guard our 'territory'.

But the importance of our feelings lies also at a deeper level. They are an essential part of life. Our well-being and our sanity depend on their balance. It is our feelings more than our thoughts which can imprison us. And one of those feelings, etched on many faces, is fear. I have now met so many who are beset by fear that I have become convinced that it deserves scrutiny.

Many fears are normal, like those that come before a big exam, an anaesthetic or a parachute jump. Fear is part of the survival mechanism of the organism. Animals will not do what is risky for them because of an instinctive fear. They have an in-built fear of those species which prey on them and will run at the sight of them. I find it a source of wonder to watch thousands of birds taking to the air from a marsh when one harrier flies over. It seems that their brains are programmed to recognise the shape of such birds of prey and fear them, and they know instinctively they are safer in the air than on the ground. So fear is helpful in certain circumstances.

People have similar instincts, but our reason enables us to override them. Yet we can be overcome by fear and destroyed by it. Fears are intended to be protective; phobias or unreasonable, exaggerated fears are destructive.

The number of things of which people can be 'unreasonably' afraid is enormous. I have seen people with fears of illness, vomiting, fainting, cancer, death; failure, not coping, breakdown; speaking in public, flying, water, crowds, open spaces, closed spaces, heights, getting lost, darkness, strangers, birds, snakes, spiders, driving alone and being alone. The incidence of these things is commoner than most realise, because there are relatively few people who admit openly to their fears.

The person who is afraid of birds cannot walk across Trafalgar Square, where thousands of pigeons roost, but will always find some reason for avoiding it: 'Let's take a taxi, I'm really quite tired.' The person who is afraid of enclosed spaces will not go in a lift: 'I always think that the exercise is good for me.' Such people require great compassion.

There are also the 'reasonable' fears. When I was quite small – about eight years old – I took my three-year-old sister to post a letter. I was allowed to do this so long as we made no attempt to cross the busy main road. Suddenly there came running towards us along the footpath a large dog, growling ferociously. I was terrified, grabbed my sister's hand and said bravely, 'Let's pray: Dear Jesus, please take this dog away.' Immediately the dog swerved, shot across the road and disappeared.

Whilst this is simply a childish memory, which reveals something about my particular background, it is still quite vivid. I have often noticed how simple experiences can have a deeper significance. It was not unreasonable to be afraid. But it was my first experience with the 'world beyond' and the truth that faith and fear are opposites. All through my life so far, I have had a tussle between faith and fear.

When I was 12 or 13, I used to go to play tennis with my friends at a local park. We were charged by the hour. But it was relatively easy to pay for an hour, play for three and escape detection. I had been brought up to be honest and I wanted to be honest. But my friends wanted to cheat and save money. I was fearful of what my friends would think: would I follow my principles or those of my friends?

This too is a child's memory, though one for which I am grateful since I did stick out for honesty. But the desire to be part of a crowd, the hatred of disagreeing with my friends, the fear of what others think of me, has been a powerful force, and I have often yielded to that fear.

At the age of eight, my faith had been built by a disappearing dog. At the age of 18, I walked the hills of Wales trying to decide what to do in life. In one sense there was nothing to decide. I had been accepted to study medicine, which I very much wanted to do. But there had come an ill-defined fear. Was there really a God? If there was, did I believe in him? If I did, what would that mean? Did he have a view on what I should do in life? Was I prepared to give my life to him? If I did that, would I continue to do medicine? Would I be able to marry? What would my friends think?

And so out of the mists of my mind arose a new fear – the fear of the unknown, the fear of trusting the God I thought I believed in. My difficulty was not that I did not believe; it was that I was not sure that I dared to believe. Yet I remember the tremendous feeling of liberation when I said yes to the God I was only beginning to know. It did not turn out to mean doing something different. It did mean doing it for a different reason.

At the age of 25, having qualified as a doctor, I was still afraid of what people thought. I prayed to be able to overcome this handicap. At the age of eight, when I prayed, the object of my fear had been removed. By 25, I had grown up and the remedy required more from me.

Shortly after my prayer, I was rung up by a much older man, a powerful figure and quite definitely feared. He asked me to come to see him. 'I'm not well,' he said. 'I'm supposed to go to South Africa. I don't think I can and would be grateful if you could come and confirm this.'

I went round and examined him. To my horror it was clear that there was nothing physically wrong with him. His symptoms arose from his own fears. He was afraid of being unwell abroad. He wanted to call off the trip and be able to say that a doctor had told him not to go.

I immediately felt panic rising within me. Supposing I said he could go and he was ill over there? But I knew that I could not be a doctor of any worth if I did not stick by my own decisions. So I took a deep breath, said that there was nothing wrong with him and advised him to go. To my surprise, he thanked me warmly and told me that I was the first doctor to be honest with him for a long time. He went and was not ill.

This broke something in me, for I have never felt the same degree of fear of people since.

I have no means of knowing how many others can identify with these stories. I tell them for two reasons. The first is that they illustrate something of a hidden journey. All of us through life are on an obvious journey. We know that we are living at a certain time and that we come from a certain place. We learn, we study, we become something – in my case a doctor. This is our natural journey through life. At the beginning there are infinite choices, but as we go on they become more limited. At the end of life we can see what we have achieved.

But the hidden journey is not perceived by everyone. It is the journey of a soul towards God. It is the awareness that life is like climbing a mountain. If we follow our conscience, if we try to follow God's ways, then our character grows. If we ignore them we wither. We can climb God's mountain or we can ignore it. We can climb and slip. We can stop. We can go round rather than up. But the first point is to recognise that it is there.

Thus these simple experiences represented hand-holds on that mountain for me.

I mention them also because these fears are experienced by

large numbers of people, and unhealed they lead not only to stunted people who are not free but to a society which is not free.

One of my sons is a bird-watcher. He likes me to take him to special sites where it is possible to see rare birds. On these trips we wear green coats and green Wellington boots. Ostensibly, this is to provide camouflage so that the birds do not fly away. But they are also signals which show that we are 'birders'. It is the old instinct to be one of a group: to be on the inside.

In a way, this is a good thing. Groups of people in many walks of life get things done. It is part of the social order; it is the reason for the buildup of nation states or ethnic groups. It is the enjoyment and protection of shared interests, shared values, shared 'language'.

But at the same time, it lies at the heart of the dilemmas of true inner freedom. Not only do groupings help to protect and cherish shared values, they also tend to enforce them; they enforce group-think. This happens in the West, not because people cannot break away; the state does not prevent them. It happens because people do not want to break away, for fear of being cast outside the circle.

I have a friend who was a Marxist. He works in industry in Birmingham. For years he espoused the Communist cause; he had turned to it originally because of a very difficult childhood. In the end, he became disillusioned and when the Party wanted to bring his factory out on strike for political reasons, and he realised that it might close the factory for good with the loss of hundreds of jobs, he broke away and persuaded the factory workers not to strike. He was immediately ostracised by his Party colleagues.

He has told me since that he felt empty and dejected. He had followed his conscience and broken away, but there was a cost. He missed the camaraderie, the sense of excitement, the purpose. For to be part of a group is rather like a drug, an addiction. If you leave, you get withdrawal symptoms. It was, if you like, the end of the old-school network in a rather tough school.

He is now one of the most constructive of trades union leaders because he is truly free and thinks independently.

Sadly that is all too rare, not just in trades union affairs but in any walk of life. When I asked one Member of Parliament, whom I greatly respect, who were the most independent-minded MPs from all parties, he replied that a list of them would not be very long.

Someone of my acquaintance was a navigator in the Royal Air Force during the Second World War, flying in Lancaster bombers. He was shot down over Germany and spent some years in a prison camp. He later worked in an office. The telephone rang. He answered it. The call was for his boss. 'Tell him I'm out.' 'Tell him yourself, Sir.'

That way does not lie promotion. My friend kept his values and his self-respect, but he lost his job. In prison he had decided that if he had the chance he would study medicine. This he finally did and spent many years as a family doctor in the North of England.

I have often reflected on those few seconds that changed the course of his life. His honesty bought his freedom. It is hard enough to be honest, but here was a young man who was prepared to put himself outside the circle, to counter the fear of standing alone.

The effect of peer group pressure varies greatly according to the nature of the group. In a healthy society, it may help to prevent those with temptations from committing crimes. But it may act equally against heroic behaviour, discouraging people from stepping out of line for good as well as evil. When Wilberforce[1] fought against the slave trade, he showed great freedom from the fear of what others thought of him; most were imprisoned in a peer grouping which accepted slavery as normal.

If society is healthy, peer group pressure can be regarded as a 'benign' cement. If society becomes malign, it can accelerate catastrophe.

Where violence occurs, it can often be seen that peer groupings play a powerful part. This is true of gang warfare or of football hooliganism, where an 'in' culture locks people into antisocial behaviour. It can also be seen in communal violence, which is so often based on 'my people right or wrong'.

A group of students from Cambridge were recruited as agents for the Soviet Union in the thirties, and remained undetected for many years, doing untold damage. Here too we see a clique which stuck together and regarded their 'group' as more important than the security of the realm.

I was very moved to go to Ireland and to meet people from all backgrounds. One Catholic doctor told me of the dilemmas of some of his patients, of the stress of families who receive a knock at the door and find the IRA there, with their guns, seeking shelter. How can they refuse? When the IRA leave, the British Army come and request information. If they do not give it they can be punished. If they do give it, the IRA may well return and shoot them. The strain is considerable.

I remember watching a television programme in America about a basketball tournament. This was a college competition and it was won by a college which had never won before, under the enthusiastic leadership of their new coach. It was a predominantly white college and he happened to be black. After they had won, the coach discovered that in the last three minutes of one match they had played a substitute who was not eligible to play, because he had not done enough studies to qualify. Unwittingly, they had cheated.

The coach, after a restless night, admitted what had happened to the authorities and they had no alternative but to strip the college of its title. The college was mortified but to its great credit supported the coach. He simply said that he could not have done anything else: 'To act differently would not have been honest.'

Considering that this occurred in the middle of the Iran Contra affair, in which it was clear that American politicians had been lying, it was a refreshingly different view of America. But there was a corollary to the story for me. Watching it, I had a sudden feeling in the pit of my stomach which indicated that my conscience had been triggered. Into my mind's eye flashed a recent incident in which I had not been honest. The result of the programme was that I went to the person concerned and told him.

It interests me that honesty is catching. But what was challenging was not just that the coach was honest, but that he was honest over something which appeared so small. He refused to cooperate with any lie. But to do so he had to overcome the fear of the opinions of all the people whom he might reasonably have been expected to want to please.

On my first visit to Poland, I went and stood silently in Warsaw beside the grave of Father Popieluszko,[2] the Polish priest who was murdered for his beliefs in 1984 – one of the latest in a long line of martyrs who have had the courage to stand against tyranny and injustice. He refused to go along with the idea that faith was a purely private affair. He refused to cooperate with untruth. His Masses 'for the nation', which attracted thousands, angered the authorities so much that he was finally killed. Now his grave has become a loved shrine. For he is one of those who helped keep Solidarity alive during the dark years. Those who knew him recognised him as a free man, someone who had defeated fear.

Both these men, the well-loved priest and the unknown basketball coach, have something important in common. They both overcame the fear of what people think. They both refused to compromise with truth. Father Popieluszko opposed a great lie. The coach refused to accept small compromises with truth. Both, as we shall see, are important in safeguarding freedom.

4   Healing the Past
– Preparing the Future

Pierre Spoerri

JUST AS THERE ARE forces in our own human nature which
resist liberation, so there are also external and historical
obstacles to freedom. The nationalisms which have
resurfaced in Eastern and Central Europe, making civil wars
actual or possible, have once again raised the question of
whether we can be free of history. Are we imprisoned by the
past or can each person and each generation start again with
a clean slate?

My father was a historian and my family upbringing taught
me to give history a central place in my view of things. World
War II broke out when I was entering high school and was a
daily reality throughout my teenage years. Shortly after the
outbreak of war, my father headed a national organisation in
Switzerland which fought the temptation of some Swiss to
submit to our powerful German neighbour. Freedom was not
then a theoretical question for us. The freedom struggles of
the Swiss, which we had read about in history, suddenly
became real. We knew that my father was on the black list
and would be arrested and even executed if the Germans
invaded.

My father-in-law, on the other hand, was a typical Baltic
baron. He came from Latvia, a country which had been
Christianised by his ancestors in the Middle Ages. After the
Russian Revolution, the Baltic landowners had been chased
away but had been able to reconquer their land with the help
of volunteers from Western Europe. As my father-in-law was
the second son of the family, the property passed to his elder
brother and he himself went to Berlin to study law. He
became a journalist and joined the German government news
agency in the twenties. In Geneva, he interviewed the big men
of the League of Nations and met his future wife. It was in

Geneva, too, that he was first faced with the challenge of National Socialism. A man from the Gestapo told him that he would not advance in his profession if he did not break off his contact with Moral Re-Armament[1] and his Christian friends.

One year before he died, he asked me whether I would be ready to listen to his life story, including the bits he was not so proud of. In those hours I discovered how many tortured nights he and many of his countrymen in similar positions must have had since the war.

While he was stationed in Vienna, the *Anschluss* (reunion) of Austria with Germany was being prepared and all opponents of Hitler's policy were moved out of the way. A friend of my father-in-law, a diplomat known for his anti-Nazi views, was forced one evening to open his door to a group of Nazi bully-boys. They filled up his bath tub with water, put his head into it and drowned him like a cat. When my father-in-law heard this the next morning, he almost went to pieces. He said to me, 'I had two young children. I did not feel I was born to be a hero. So I decided to bend rather than to break. I have wondered ever since whether this was the moment when I took the wrong turning in my life.'

When, in the summer of 1990, my wife told this story to two senior Soviet newspapermen, one of them was so moved that he could hardly talk. The other said, 'We have gone through a similar experience. Stalin was as much of an evil genius for us as Hitler was for you. Our grandchildren are now asking us, "Why didn't you do anything when Stalin was terrorising the country?" We say, of course, that we didn't know everything that was going on. But I knew that an innocent man down our street was picked up in the middle of the night and didn't come back. And we didn't do anything.'

Because those directly affected by National Socialism, Hitler and World War II are slowly but steadily becoming a minority, many imagine that the next generations in Europe will be able to live life less weighed down by the past. But is it really true that time alone cures everything, and that after a number of years the wounds of the past will be automatically healed?

Experience shows that this is not necessarily so. Whether they like it or not, many German men and women who had nothing to do with various painful events of their nation's history are still affected by them. When I met a young German who had gone as an exchange student to California, he told me that on his return he had asked his mother, 'Will I have to apologise all my life for being a German?' Almost every week during his time in the United States, films were shown on television in which the Germans – usually SS officers – were the 'baddies'. These films had influenced the attitude of the young Americans towards him, a young German. The boy's mother, an historian herself, answered, 'No, you don't have to apologise for being a German, because you weren't born when Hitler did what he did. But as a responsible citizen, you will have to live with our history and accept its consequences.'

The French historian Alfred Grosser writes in his book *Le Crime et la mémoire* (The Crime and the Memory): 'Since the 1950s, every time the Germans have complained that on French television their country is shown only as the Third Reich and an occupying power, it has been necessary to stress the fact that it was less the French image of Germany that was the problem than the difficulty for us French to take responsibility for what we ourselves had done between 1940 and 1944. The *Vergangenheitsbewältigung* (facing up to the past) which since the war has been a constant subject of discussion in the German Federal Republic, has only slowly become a conscious issue in France.'[2]

One of the avowed tasks of the President of Germany at the time of her re-unification, Richard von Weizsäcker, is to give history its rightful place: 'Contemporary history should not be suppressed, but neither should it be made into an ideology nor used as a political instrument. The better we manage this, the more likely it is that the historical roots which are common to us in East and West will lead to peace and not to danger for the future. The younger generation need to contribute to this task too. They are not responsible for what happened then, but they are responsible for what history will make out of it.'[3]

Alfred Grosser stresses in his book the role that professors of history in different countries have played in establishing a common view – and a common teaching – of history. Soon after the Second World War, the German-American school book conferences reached agreement relatively quickly on a common perspective of history. 'The German-French agreement of 1953', Grosser adds, 'allowed without great difficulty a common and detailed formulation of the origins of the 1914-18 war and clear statements about 1939 and the Hitler regime. Only the origins of baroque art remained a problem...'[4] The French made an unprecedented gesture: the head of the French historical archives asked a German historian to write the first volume of a new national history of France.[5] School-book conferences between German and Polish and between German and Soviet historians have been slowly making progress, although they have practically been overtaken by events in Eastern Europe since 1989.

The distinguished columnist James Reston wrote in 1986, a few years before the major changes in Eastern Europe: 'History does not support the notion of inevitable and endless conflict between states of competing philosophies... As in the religious wars that went on for centuries, problems that seemed insoluble were finally resolved between France and Germany, the United States and Japan.'[6] One international relationship which has altered and has stabilised in its new form for the last 40 years is, as Reston says, the relationship between France and Germany.

It is hardly necessary to describe the feelings between the people of these two great European powers as they contested for continental and world power in the second half of the nineteenth and the first half of the twentieth centuries. Millions of Germans and French died on the battlefields of three major wars in the course of 70 years. Leaders and ordinary citizens could not help but feel that their countries were hereditary enemies and that this would remain so till the end of time.

Two events in 1946 were symbols of a new beginning. When Frank Buchman, an American, arrived in Switzerland in June 1946 to open a World Assembly for Moral Re-Armament and discovered that no Germans were present, he stunned the Europeans by saying, 'Where are the Germans? You will never rebuild Europe without the Germans.'[7] And he did not leave it at that. Within days,

emissaries were on their way to the Western capitals and then
to Germany. And within four months, the first major group
of Germans to be allowed to leave their country had arrived
in Switzerland.

The same year, in September, Winston Churchill made his
famous speech at my father's university in Zurich. He gave
his vision of the future of Europe, and then said, 'The first
step in the recreation of the European family must be a
partnership between France and Germany... There can be no
revival of Europe without a spiritually great France and a
spiritually great Germany... In all this urgent work, France
and Germany must take the lead together... Great Britain, the
British Commonwealth of Nations, mighty America, and I
trust Soviet Russia – for then indeed all would be well – must
be friends and sponsors of the new Europe and must
champion its right to live and shine.'[8]

The French writer Léon Bloy once said, 'Prophets are men
who remember the future.' It was hardly possible for
Churchill or Buchman to know in 1946 that by 1986
Germany and France, their leaders, their peoples and their
younger generation would be so closely linked that a conflict
between the two countries would be considered an
impossibility even by the greatest of pessimists. A symbolic
gesture marked this new relationship in September 1984
when Germany's Chancellor Helmut Kohl met the French
President, François Mitterrand, on the battlefield of Verdun
where more than one million German and French soldiers
had died during World War I. The declaration of the two men
was very simple: 'We became reconciled. We started to
understand each other. We have become friends.'

In the Europe of the nineties, the relations between
Germany and her neighbours in the East and between the
East and South-East European nations themselves will
determine the future of the whole region. For thousands of
Germans who had to leave their ancestral lands and flee for
their lives with their families at the end of World War II –
their numbers are estimated at 15 million, of whom at least
two million died on the roads[9] – some declarations have
helped to heal bitter memories of the past. President Václav
Havel of Czechoslovakia spoke on several occasions with

deep regret of the terrible events after the surrender of the Germans in 1945. He said, 'We have a duty to apologise to the Germans who were expelled after the Second World War.'[10] He was supported by the head of the Catholic Church, Cardinal Frantisek Tomasek who ended his declaration by saying: 'Truth and love will make us free.'[11]

It was a pioneering step of the Polish bishops that opened the way to a new relationship between the Germans and the Poles. In their historic letter of 18 November, 1965, they wrote to their German colleagues, 'And despite everything, despite this situation that is almost hopelessly burdened with the past, we call on you, highly esteemed brothers, to come out and away from precisely that situation: let us try to forget!... We grant forgiveness and we ask your forgiveness.'[12] The German bishops answered in the same spirit, and there were several meetings between the leaders of both churches in the years that followed.

At the beginning of October 1986, the Polish writer Wladislaw Bartoszewski received the Peace Prize of the German Book Fair in Frankfurt. It was a symbolic gesture of reconciliation, as Bartoszewski had been in the first group of Polish intellectuals to be taken to the death-camp of Auschwitz. Through an extraordinary set of circumstances – or miracles – his life had been saved. When receiving the prize, Bartoszewski said, 'If in the winter of 1940 somebody had said to me that in the course of one lifetime the overwhelming majority of Germans would change into a society guided by humanitarian principles and into an accepted constitutionally established European state and parliamentary democracy, I would have considered this the optimistic dream of a utopian ... And even if one can discuss whether and how far the thinking in stereotypes of Germans about Poles and of Poles about Germans has been overcome, this celebration today seems a not wholly insignificant event on the way to the kind of changes which give rise to hope.'[13]

One of the most dramatic events in terms of national reconciliation since the Second World War was probably the visit of the Polish Prime Minister, Tadeusz Mazowiecki, to the Katyn Forest in the western part of the Soviet Union. This tragic story started in 1939 when after the occupation of

Poland by Hitler and Stalin, 15,000 Polish officers were taken prisoner and disappeared in camps in the Soviet Union. The graves of 5,000 of them were discovered by the Germans when they invaded Byelorussia. But it was only in 1989 that the Soviet authorities admitted that a special KGB commando unit had been responsible for all these deaths. It was not only the killings but the systematic denials of them for so long that poisoned Polish-Russian relations for 50 years.

Katyn was the most important stopping point on Prime Minister Mazowiecki's first official visit to the Soviet Union. He was accompanied on this journey by the Deputy Prime Minister of the Soviet government, Laviorov. Kneeling in front of the monument of Katyn, Mazowiecki just said six words: 'Lord, give them your eternal peace.' The Dominican Father who read the requiem Mass added, 'The frontier between good and evil does not run between states, not even between people, but straight through the heart of each one of us.'[14]

To heal the past in order to prepare the future is not a job reserved for specialists. It is one that concerns us all. The same shaft of light which reveals with an amazing clarity, if we are ready for it, our own past as individuals and as peoples can also illumine the steps that will lead us all into a new future.

5 The Way to Forgiveness and Reconciliation

Pierre Spoerri

AT THE END of World War II there were not only bitter relationships between European nations to heal. The same was also necessary in Asia. The transformation of the relationship between Japan and its wartime enemies was as dramatic as the Franco-German reconciliation. As a young student I watched the arrival in Switzerland, in the summer of 1950, of the first large delegation of Japanese to visit the West after the war. This group included several Members of Parliament from different parties, amongst them the youngest Member of the Diet at that time, Yasuhiro Nakasone. (He announced that he would be Prime Minister of his country 'in 20 years' time'. As it happened, it took him 30 years to reach his goal.)

For me, the two most impressive figures were the Lord Mayors of Hiroshima and Nagasaki. The Mayor of Hiroshima brought with him some wooden crosses made out of the remnants of a 400-year-old camphor tree which had been standing at the heart of the city when the first atom bomb exploded. He was a man of few words. When he returned to his city the wording on the monument remembering the men and women killed by the bomb was changed on his initiative. Instead of underlining the desire to remember what had been done to them for the rest of time, the inscription now reads, 'Sleep in peace. We shall never make the same mistake again.'

In 1957, in the Philippines, a group of senior political leaders of Japan – the colonial power from 1910 until the end of World War II – met with their counterparts from Korea at an international conference for Moral Re-Armament. The Japanese newspaper *Yomiuri* wrote of the 'beginning of a solution to the Japanese-Korean problem': 'In particular, the

43

apology made by Mr. Hoshijima (later the Speaker of the Japanese Diet) and Mrs. Kato ... for the oppression used by the Japanese during the time of their rule in Korea seems to have met with a great response in Korea...'[1] It took another 30 years till, on the occasion of an official visit of South Korea's President Roh Tae Woo to Japan, the Japanese Emperor spoke words that were meant to put a final end to the long-standing dispute: 'I think of the sufferings your people underwent during this unfortunate period, which were brought about by my country, and cannot but feel the deepest regret.'[2]

The same group of Japanese who met the Koreans conferred also with their hosts, the leaders of the Philippines. The effect of the Japanese apology was immediate. In less than six months an accord including reparations, diplomatic recognition and the establishment of trade relations was completed. When the Filipino President Garcia visited Tokyo in December 1958 he declared over Japanese television, 'Our ideological and geographical affinities are strong bonds that should hold us together in lasting friendship and enduring peace. It may be truthfully said that the bitterness of former years is being washed away by compassion and forgiveness.'[3]

But in Asia there are also relationships that go back much further than the last World War. When I talked to one of the advisers of the Dalai Lama, the exiled ruler of Tibet, he told us of his attempt to get some of the minority groups who now live under Chinese rule, to sit together at the same table. He started with a group from Mongolia and East Turkestan. (The East Turkestanis are Muslims and live in the western-most province of China, Sinkiang). But the East Turkestanis voiced strong objections to a suggestion that representatives from Manchuria should be included. Several centuries ago the Manchus had ruled East Turkestan with a cruel hand: they had killed and tortured thousands of scholars and ordinary people, and virtually enslaved the whole nation.

Similarly, when the Mongols wanted to bring to the talks a scholar who happened to be Chinese, protests erupted again. The understanding had been that the meeting was only for people who had suffered under the Chinese – from Mongolia,

Tibet, Manchuria and East Turkestan – as most of those present wanted to concentrate on discussing how 'big brother' China had ill-treated them all. In dealing with Chinese, Mongol, Manchu and Tibetan history, reactions, experiences and prejudices surface which go back many centuries.

In this case, the representative of the Dalai Lama had himself experienced a profound change of attitude a few months before the meeting. Having lost four members of his family because of the occupation of Tibet, he had never responded to the Dalai Lama's attempts to start a dialogue with Peking. But when he had told his story to a group of Asians, which included some young Chinese, two of them made a heart-felt apology for what their people had done to Tibet. This so moved him that it enabled him to look squarely at his own bitterness and become free of it. At the meeting of the minorities, he was able to use this experience to help to bring the opposing groups together, with the result that they too apologised to each other and then decided to face the challenges of the future side by side.

Looking at these examples – and many more which could be described – some common elements can be discerned as steps to enable anybody to have a part in this historic process. On a visit to Jerusalem, which also lies in the heart of a region of conflicts, I heard a religious personality, living in Jerusalem, highlight three steps needed in any reconciliation: first, both sides need to admit that they have harmed one another; second, they must commit themselves to seeking a solution based on justice and not on violence, as any solution imposed by force will not be permanent; third, as there is no absolute justice, each side must determine what it will be ready to sacrifice to allow a solution.

In his paper on *Track Two Diplomacy* the American diplomat Joseph Montville also speaks of three steps that are necessary in this kind of conflict resolution: '1) humanising relations among adversary leaders; 2) improving the public environment for peacemaking; 3) building cooperative economic development schemes which institutionalise the revolutionary new peaceful relationship between the countries involved.'[4]

The third of these steps is clearly one in which governments have the principal role to play. In the consolidation of the new Franco-German relationship, for instance, it was the Schuman Plan, linking the steel and coal industries of Germany and France, which represented the point of no return. In his often-quoted letter of 9 May, 1950, to Chancellor Adenauer, the French Foreign Minister Robert Schuman wrote, 'The elimination of the age-old opposition of France and Germany, and a pooling of resources and production, will make war between the two countries not merely unthinkable but actually impossible.'

Of course, neither the goodwill of both sides nor the ingenious plan would have worked without the massive capital inflow provided by the Marshall Plan, which in itself was the institutional fruit of a change of thinking in government and in public opinion in that whole nation.

The 'philosopher' of the Schuman Plan, Jean Monnet, expressed the link between a change of attitude in the individual and the institution: 'Experience begins over again with every person. Institutions alone become wiser; they accumulate the general experience and from their experience and this wisdom come the rules which, once people have accepted them, change gradually not their nature, but their behaviour.'[5]

However in the first two steps mentioned by Montville a change in behaviour and a change in the deeper motivation in people are implicit. Four active principles are part of this process:

* the capacity to apologise;
* the readiness to forgive and even to forget;
* the ability of true compassion to slip into another person's skin;
* the decision to move into positive action with the former adversary.

In a *Time* essay dealing with the issue of personal and national repentance, Charles Krauthammer wrote, 'There is a wisdom beyond sentimentality in the authentic apology. For an individual or a society, that capacity is a sign of life, of vitality, of a soul that can still be moved...a society capable of authentic feeling.. that possesses a vitality that dead societies have lost and a discipline that mobilised societies have forfeited.'[6]

There have been 'historic' apologies like the one extended by Chancellor Adenauer to the Prime Minister of Luxemburg, Josef Bech, after World War II; or the apologies expressed by Japanese leaders like Prime Minister Kishi during the same period to Asian leaders and countries. Another apology of historical dimensions was the one extended by the French resistance leader and politician, Irène Laure, to the Germans in the summer of 1947, an apology that the Frenchwoman repeated on German soil many times in the years that followed. It was the kind of audacious action that prepared, more than any official statements, the 'public environment for peacemaking' between Germany and France.

A similar apology was extended in the summer of 1986 at a conference in Switzerland by a Turkish professor to the Greeks and Armenians present. The Turk took the trouble to invite the Greeks and Armenians to tell him what his people had done to their people in the course of the past decades. The apology was accepted, as the desire to identify with the failures of the past was genuine and heartfelt. It was a unique occasion, and even men who do not easily shed tears were visibly moved by the occasion.

What do you do when somebody extends an apology to you? What is the right response?

An Irish politician once said, 'Half of our problem is the people who cannot forgive and forget, and half the people who cannot remember.' The three words forgive, forget and remember are closely linked. The 1989 Nobel Peace Prize winner, Elie Wiesel, feels deeply that the main task of those who escaped the hell of Auschwitz is to help everybody to remember. When asked whether his concept of peace included also the notion of forgiveness, he said that even if as a person he could forgive, as he did not believe in collective guilt he did not feel he had the right to offer collective forgiveness either.

But there are other examples in history. The delegates to the peace conference of Osnabrück in 1648 after the Thirty Years War pledged *oblivio perpetua et amnestia* (forgiveness and eternal forgetting). At the end of that war, Europe was lying in ruins. Only one in three Germans had survived and Germany seemed doomed for generations to come. Michael Stürmer, the German historian of that period, comments, 'It was Christian forgiveness that was offered and accepted. Those present met each other on the basis of knowing that no man is without failings. In addition, the people concerned knew that it was political realism to recognise that you miss the future if you do not deal with the past. "Forgiveness and eternal forgetting" does not mean allowing yourself the luxury of hiding in silence and refusing to know. It means the difficult art of peacemaking, without which there is no end and also no beginning.'[7]

The process of the transformation of a relationship – be it personal or national – from hatred and mistrust through indifference to trust and love, is a continual one. It does not necessarily help to look only at each other and become fascinated by one particular relationship. True Franco-German teamwork did not arise when Germans and French gathered to talk about German and French affairs. Rather it developed as they discussed the common tasks which would demand the best from both countries and both peoples. At one international meeting, a German suggested that their experiences together could be used with people from India and Pakistan to help them build together a new kind of South Asia. Men and women with this kind of experience may become an essential element of diplomacy in the post-Berlin Wall world.

6   Are we Free to Choose?

Pierre Spoerri

IF NATIONS CAN be imprisoned by history, are we also victims of our own personal past? Are we in reality free to choose? 'Why does X have difficulties at school? Why is Mrs Y always so depressed? Why has Mr Z become an alcoholic? Wherever such questions are discussed today, a theory is inevitably brought forward which has become an absolute certainty for many people, that the root is to be found in some unpleasant experience in early childhood.' Thus provocatively the scientific editor of the German weekly *Die Zeit* Dieter E. Zimmer, opens a series of articles on 'the so-called unconscious'.[1] Zimmer adds that it has become an almost general belief – he calls it a 'pseudo-doctrine' – that all of us are inevitably prisoners of our early childhood, that these experiences not only determine our whole lives but that they also absolve us from having to take full responsibility for our present actions: in the final analysis we are not responsible.

Of course we cannot dismiss the potent and lasting effect of childhood experiences. It is part of the process of becoming an adult to discover which of these have hurt or harmed us. Sometimes professional help is needed to uncover hurts which have been deliberately forgotten. There is also a wider dimension. Nobody who saw the pictures of the faces of Romanian children 'brought up' in Ceausescu's so-called children's homes will underestimate what total neglect and lack of human care can do to young human souls. The effect of such an inhuman policy will be discovered only as its victims grow up.

Where Zimmer may have a point is that 'pseudo-doctrines' have become part of the thinking of many contemporary men and women, especially over whether we as individual human beings have freedom of choice and are responsible for our actions. For many people, this is a theoretical question of little interest. For those who are totally absorbed by the sheer

fight for survival, to debate the issue of 'choice' is a luxury
which they cannot afford. Others, absorbed by day-to-day life
with its fascination, interest, pleasure and stimulation, do not
seem to be affected by deeper issues. But for many, a personal
crisis – perhaps illness, the death of a close relative, professional failure, or fear and disillusion – starts the search for
answers to some of these existential questions.

The historian Paul Johnson writes in *A History of the
Modern World*, 'Marx, Freud, Einstein all conveyed the same
message to the 1920s: the world was not what it seemed...
Moreover, Marxist and Freudian analysis combined to under-
mine, in their different ways, the highly developed sense of
personal responsibility, and of duty towards a settled and
objectively true moral code, which was at the centre of
nineteenth-century European civilisation.'[2]

Johnson adds, 'Mistakenly but perhaps inevitably, relativity
became confused with relativism. No one was more distressed
than Einstein by this public misapprehension... Einstein was
not a practising Jew, but he acknowledged a God. He believed
passionately in absolute standards of right and wrong.'
Analysing Karl Marx's thinking, Johnson writes, 'On the
surface, men appeared to be exercising their free will, taking
decisions, determining events. In reality... such individuals,
however powerful, were seen to be mere flotsam, hurled hither
and thither by the irresistible surges of economic forces...'[3]

The arguments for relativism would not hold such fascination if they did not represent at least a half-truth. This is also
true of the theory that we are 'prisoners of history', that each
personality is determined not only by his own personal
experiences but also by those of his people, class, caste or
language group. Here, too, past experiences can be used as an
explanation. Nobody can blame anybody for hating an
oppressor who has made their people suffer for decades on
end; and for too many, such suffering is not a theory but a
painful daily reality.

It is, however, a common failing of human nature to look for
excuses. One classic excuse is to give to the other person or
other group – especially the opposing group – the stamp of a
collective character: the Swiss are materialistic, money-loving,
humourless; the British are like this, the whites or the blacks

are like that. This psychological process helps to excuse our own reactions, and at the same time focusses attention on the weak points of the other person or the other group.

This kind of argument, by which modern man feels tempted to limit his responsibility for his own actions, has been in existence for quite some time. Some of the latest discoveries in psychology, however, indicate that the individual person does have plenty of space to shape his own life and destiny, whatever his origins may be. Several American psychologists, for instance, have been able to show that children who had serious difficulties in their early years are in no way condemned to a traumatic life afterwards.

The psychologist Jean MacFarlane, in a study covering a period of 40 years, writes, 'Many of the most mature adults in the whole group, many of the most effective and creative individuals who had clear principles, much understanding and who accepted themselves and other people, were actually those who had lived through very difficult situations in their youth...' On the other hand, there were those who had been the lucky ones, who had no serious problems during their education and who had been the most competent and talented. 'At the age of 30, a high percentage of dissatisfied, helpless and rather rotten adults were found among them, whose potential had not been fulfilled, at least not up to that point.'

MacFarlane concludes, 'All these studies and many more point in one and the same direction: The adult is not condemned to continue on the road started in his childhood ... He can overcome it ... On the other hand, the absence of crises in early years does not protect from later problems!'[4]

Recent discoveries in evolution and microbiology have also added new angles. The traditional argument of determinism based on Darwin's discoveries proposed that man was a result of chance. The development from lower forms of life to higher, according to this argument, was inevitable and uncontrollable. *Homo sapiens* was just one result of this evolution; many other results could also have been possible.

More recent scientific discussions have produced further questions. Are we really only the products and even the slaves of our genes? Are we what we are, and do we do what we do, because we are determined by our genes? Microbiologists would be the first to say that the genes neither hinder nor help the everyday process of individual decision-making. The provocative title of a recent book *The Selfish Gene*[5] seems to indicate that a gene is capable of moral decisions. Reading the book, one discovers that the author did not mean this at all. He certainly would have agreed with an even more recent study that said, 'The genes control only some very elementary chemical processes in a largely determinist way; but even at this level their activity is subject to spontaneous variation, and manifold influence and control from surrounding conditions... The genes only determine the framework, the frontier inside which the influences of the surroundings and of learning experiences can modify behaviour...'[6]

At a party in Bonn, a professor of microbiology from the University tried to explain to me his latest experiments, and constantly ran into the difficulty of being unable to make himself understood to a non-specialist. He is doing research on the life and development of 'archae-bacteria', a kind of microbe which represents a form of life roughly 3,000 million years old. What makes these microbes particularly interesting is that they allow the study of the transition from inorganic to organic matter and therefore also the process of photo-synthesis.[7]

By the end of the conversation scientist and layman agreed on two basic points. The first was that microbiology and related sciences may well soon be able to explain a single step of evolution. The latest discoveries in the field of communication inside the cell and between cells indicate that this moment is not so far away. The second was that if the day comes when a step of evolution can be not only explained but induced, this will still not explain the mystery of the *direction* of evolution. The fact that even the more primitive living things were endowed with the ability to develop into something higher, and that finally human beings with consciousness and conscience evolved, seems almost easier to explain with the master-plan of a Creator than with the concept of pure 'chance and necessity'.

This is finally a question of personal faith. The winner of the Nobel Prize for Physics and General Director of the

European Nuclear Research Centre (CERN), Charles Rubia, said in an interview: 'Religion has to do with the inner man. I do not think that listening to the signals of nature can give us an answer to the signals coming from our inner man. Counting the galaxies or proving the existence of elementary particles is probably no proof of the existence of God. But as a researcher I am profoundly impressed by the order and the beauty which I see in the cosmos and in the interior of matter. And as an observer of nature I cannot deny the idea that there is a pre-existing order of things. The idea that all this should be the result of chance, of a sheer statistical variation, is for me totally unacceptable. There must be an intelligence which is on a higher level than the existence of the universe.'[8]

In a similar way the writer Thomas Mann said in a radio talk in a series called *This I believe*: 'In the depth of my soul I believe – and consider this belief to be natural to any human soul – that this earth has a central significance in the universe. In the depth of my soul I entertain the presumption that the act of creation which called forth the inorganic world from nothingness, and the procreation of life from the inorganic world, was aimed at humanity. A great experiment was initiated, whose failure by human irresponsibility would mean the failure of the act of creation itself, its very refutation. Maybe it is so, maybe it is not. It would be good if humanity behaved as if it were so.'[9]

Several aspects of this 'great experiment' will demand an urgent and serious study in the present generation. One is the question how the population of the globe will be kept on a level which will not increase the danger of poverty and hunger in the developing countries and the resulting North-South tension. It is an issue which touches on the freedom and responsibility of the individual as well as on the development of whole countries and continents. In the industrial countries there is an increasing number of people who for many reasons do not want to be burdened with the raising of children. In the poorer countries, a great number of children still mean a greater security for old age. The issue is so complex that a solution – acceptable both for the individual and valid for mankind – may only be found if the best of scientists and spiritual leaders get together to work on it.

The giants of nuclear science of the thirties and forties had fundamental discussions on many of these issues while they were discovering some of the secrets of life which today are almost taken for granted. Two of these men, Einstein and the Danish nuclear physicist Bohr, had profound disagreements. A great German scientist of the post-war era, Professor C.F. von Weizsäcker, wrote on Einstein's hundredth birthday, 'The origin of the conflict was whether the classic form of physical determinism had to be sacrificed in favour of physical predictions based on probabilities. "God does not throw dice," said Einstein, and Bohr replied, "The question is not whether God throws dice, but whether we know what we mean when we say that God does not throw dice." The real issue concerned the concept of physical reality. Einstein saw in this reality something objective, which can be thought out "independently of what one perceives through one's senses". Bohr had ... already moved to the concept that all science is our science, a science of man.'[10]

Meanwhile, similar discussions are going on concerning *artificial intelligence* (AI). Since this term was created in 1956 at the Dartmouth Conference, the first wave of apprehension in the general public has come and gone. Of course there have been science fiction authors – like Martin Caidin in *The God Machine* – who have described electronic brains which aspire to dominate the world. But the serious researchers seem to know the limitations of the machines they are producing. One of them wrote in the summer of 1990, 'We do not want machines which share with us their mistakes and moods. We want machines which free us from jobs for which we are not so well suited. (By accepting such a restriction) we may lose a dream today, but we shall gain by preserving the sense of wonder about ourselves.'[11]

This is expressed in different terms by Professor Valentin Braitenberg, Director of the Max Planck Institute for biological cybernetics in Tübingen. Speaking of his research into the workings of the human brain, Braitenberg says, 'What is interesting is that the actual functions of the brain are much more effective and intelligent than anything that we can invent to explain them... I am never disappointed when I have to revise my own ideas again and again, as I learn something better every time.'[12]

What can we conclude from these scientific observations? Each human being, especially each adult, carries a considerable pack of experience, of personal and collective history, on his back. But whether this pack crushes him down or is a relatively light weight on his shoulders, is largely up to him to decide. And each person is free to steadily increase his area of freedom.

The process of becoming free has been brilliantly described by the Swiss psychiatrist Paul Tournier: 'We assert ourselves as persons in the moment of choice freely and responsibly made: then life wells up in us. Thereafter it sinks gradually back into the automatisms it has created and which become our prison. ... True liberty flows, then, from our being freed from automatism. To be free is to become oneself once more, not the biological self of reflexes, of inexorable mechanisms that impede the flow of life, but the self of the person.'[13]

Do the 'automatisms' mentioned by Tournier still control us, or are we actually able to decide 'freely and responsibly'? Becoming more conscious of the 'Self', described by Tournier, is an essential step to inner freedom.

We all face major choices in life over profession and marriage, for example. Most of us come to decisive moments when to take a stand on principles we believe in would jeopardise our careers or future chances in life. Are we governed by circumstances? Do our desires dictate our decisions? What other forces can deflect us from the path we have set ourselves?

7 What is Success Worth?

John Lester

ONE OF THE powerful motivating forces in human nature is the desire for success, which also raises the question of how we measure worth. Looking back on preceding centuries it is obvious that all over Europe, certain families achieved great power. Simply to be a member of one of these families was more significant than anything any individual in the family might actually do. Worth was thought to be dependent on breeding. Class bitterness arose from this inequality and has marked our own century in a major way.

Today's society has different values but is not necessarily more equal. We have largely replaced the idea of worth dependent on breeding with the thought that it derives from succeeding. Aristocracy has ceded much of its power to meritocracy.

The worth of an individual measured by success does not primarily depend on the object of that success. We give roughly equal merit to the successful scientist, pop-star, sportsman or politician. The merit lies in the ability to succeed. In Britain acclaim was even given by many to the 'great mail-train robbers', a gang which held up a mail-train and escaped with a huge sum of money, leaving the guard to die later of his injuries. The ability to produce folk heroes from such a crime reveals what it means to make a god of success.

Yet most people would still accept that certain tasks – usually those of service to the community – have a special worth: we are grateful to teachers and to nurses. They lie, nonetheless, at the bottom of any pay-scale and in a totally different league from a successful tennis-player. Whilst we admire those who serve others, we reward those who seek success for themselves.

The inequality caused by class division provoked great anger because no one could choose what family they were born into; but present secular society is producing an equally unbalanced sense of worth. While it is true that freedom allows people to develop their talents, so that they can rise by their own efforts, it is also true that talents are as arbitrary as the privileges of birth. They are not distributed equally. Individuals are not equal in ability. For someone to succeed in a competitive society usually implies that someone else must fail. There are plenty of people who have not been gifted with the talents needed for a competitive society. What is the worth of a loser?

The search for an egalitarian society is an understandable one: but it is a superficial response to what may in reality be a more fundamental question. Nowhere has it been marked by success. For if we are to have freedom then we have the freedom to achieve, to maximise what we have been arbitrarily given, and that increases diversity and disparity. It is only by restricting freedom that we can, artificially, create a more egalitarian society.

Yet the results of such manipulation have been catastrophic. Hitler ended up murdering millions of Jews because he thought they were worthless; he only served to diminish humanity through that appalling crime. In the Soviet Union, their experiment succeeded in destroying people's sense of dignity and worth, through the removal by murder of millions of citizens in Stalin's purges, the locking-up of difficult people who disagreed with declared 'truths', and the production of a new élite of privileged Party people ending in a society which stagnated and finally broke down.

If totalitarian societies produce conformity and deadness, diminishing the value and creativity of the individual, and if liberal societies produce an ever greater disparity with some apparently succeeding and others apparently failing, then where is the true meaning of worth to be found? For the desire to form an egalitarian society arises out of the instinctive feeling that all people are fundamentally equal in worth.

In Communist societies, those who sought to reach the top had, of necessity, to cooperate with the system and with the lie at the heart of it. They accepted untruth in their souls, which imprisoned and diminished them. Yet they 'apparently' succeeded.

Those who refused to cooperate, who stuck to the truth at great personal cost were ostracised and penalised for it. They 'apparently' failed. But they retained their dignity and inner liberty and were then in a position to restore the worth of their peoples.

It is in these deeper values of life that the meaning of true worth is to be found. Life's journey for all of us has its easy and its difficult moments. The failures and struggles are as important to the growth of character as the successes, and often more interesting.

On a visit to America I stayed in the home of a very fine family. He was a lawyer, she was equally able. They were in their thirties and had three energetic young sons. He was a partner in one of the best legal firms in Washington, and his ambition was to be the best lawyer in America. They had everything made except for one thing. He had developed cancer.

He knew that although medically qualified I was only doing a little medical work because I was giving my time voluntarily with Moral Re-Armament. 'I could never do that,' he said. 'I could never give up my career, never give up law.' For me it was a poignant moment. I could see that the cancer had a grip on him so that, barring the unforeseen, he would not only have to give up law but life itself.

They were Christians and had been praying for a miracle. I have seen people make a full recovery who medically speaking should not have got better, so I could share in their hope. It requires faith to believe; it requires even more faith to realise that God may not intend a miracle, and to submit fully to whatever he allows.

It was this thought that I tried to communicate – for it was clear that he was nearer the end than any of the family had dared to face. Before he died some six weeks later, that gift was given, that lifting of the burden of his ambition. He died at peace knowing that his worth to God was not measured by his achievements. He had fought a good fight against his disease and lost. But at a deeper level he had won. He had been granted a deep sense of the presence of God.

Today many are afraid of death, afraid even of thinking about it. If life is all about achieving, or if merit is measured in terms of competition, then death renders it hollow. If worth depends on success, then someone who is smitten down before they have the chance to succeed is rendered worthless. If all we are interested in or believe in lies in the realm of the material, death remains the end of everything. We need an experience, a philosophy of life, which makes sense of the great unknown.

My wife and I have two sons. When the younger one was born there were complications. We were told by the doctors that he would probably be deaf, blind and retarded. As a doctor I could see the logic of what was presented to us. But as a father the pain was very heavy. Having felt desperately worried, a simple thought freed both my wife and me. It was that accepting Christ, which we had both done, is not an insurance against pain or suffering, but rather a promise that God will be with us in our pain.

Wonderfully for our son and for us, this story had a happy ending. The doctors' prognostications proved ill-founded; he has had a few minor difficulties to overcome, but nothing serious. But in retrospect we are grateful for the experience. For it taught us compassion for those who suffer in the long term and it revealed to us that love and worth have nothing to do with ability.

These simple experiences reveal to me the reality of deeper truths: that God does not love me because of any talents he may have given me, but because he is love and because he loves each one of us: that every life, every soul, is unique and of great worth to him.

Worth in this sense lies in the fact that life itself is a gift, that it has an intrinsic worth. Worth thus emerges as part of the value system which produces absolute values – for each life has an absolute value. Parents who suffer the misfortune of a stillbirth or a cot-death are sometimes encouraged by their friends to have another child as soon as possible 'to replace the one they have lost'. Those who have suffered such losses never see it like that. They know that no life is replaceable by another; every single life is unique and in that lies its worth.

But in addition it is clear that each one of us has the opportunity to develop, for our spirit and our character to grow. Such growth does not depend on success, though success may result from it, but arises from the choices we make.

When Maximilian Kolbe, the Polish priest, offered during the Second World War to take the place of a prisoner who had been condemned to die, because the condemned man had a family to look after, he removed his own opportunity for survival and for future success. Yet everyone – religious or not – recognises the 'worth' in this sacrifice, that such a choice is of much greater value than superficial success. It is because we can recognise this that he is remembered long after most of his contemporaries have been forgotten.

But if we begin to see a different meaning for the quality of worth, then what about equality? For it is clear that on this basis every one of us can and should be equal, but we often do not feel that way.

Our family lived for some years in Birmingham and our elder boy went to a Catholic inner-city comprehensive school. Many of the boys were the sons of working-class Irish fathers. I thought I was free of prejudice and was quite happy with the school until the language, accents, culture and attitudes of the boys began to rub off on to my son. I was concerned that the school was spoiling his 'Englishness'.

We were then invited to a Mass at the school for parents and boys, and as I sat there – English and professional among many less academic parents and children – I was in turmoil because, in spite of myself, I despised them. I did not mind my son associating with them, but I did not want him to become one of them. Something akin to hatred of what they might do to our family welled up in my heart. Yet we were supposed to be taking Communion together.

Suddenly I saw that that would be hypocrisy. I sensed Jesus saying, 'I died for them as well as you. I love them as well as you. Why do you not love them?' For me it was a choice. I had liked to think of myself as balanced, objective and unprejudiced, but I had suddenly seen that deep down there were very unpleasant streams which needed cleansing.

I can now say that true equality came as we knelt at the altar before God. Aware of my own need I realised for the first time that equality has everything to do with the need of forgiveness. At that moment a great weight of unrecognised and unjustified superiority was taken from me, and affection took its place. This has grown steadily, and I began to see the enormous debt we owe to Ireland for the faith and education which it has contributed to Europe and far beyond.

Whilst lack of freedom is detrimental to self-worth and to society, and whilst it is clear that much richer developments can occur in freedom, so too we can recognise that freedom can be used in ways which in the end threaten it.

Freedom allows us to follow our natural desires; to consider it normal to use our talents to benefit ourselves; to increase our wealth and power; to enjoy a competitive, acquisitive society. The danger is that we can regard that as the only logical outcome of freedom, the true fruits of the free society.

But mankind is also free to choose the ways of God, which have remained valid for centuries: to accept absolute values, to accept that the gift of great talents offers the opportunity for great service: to create a society which regards every life, whether brilliant or blemished, as of equal worth in the sight of God and therefore infinitely precious.

Faith-filled concepts have lost momentum in this century, not because they have been found to be false but simply because people have been conditioned by the all-pervasiveness of secular values into thinking that society is secular and selfish, and that religion should be regarded only as a private affair.

If life is really all about drive and ability leading to success and achievement, then some people will certainly reach the top. To succeed is not of itself a bad thing. It may benefit society greatly, but it can never be satisfying as the final goal. The development of the soul, of the inner being, does not depend on ability: it depends on obedience and faithfulness to conscience and to the 'heavenly vision'. It is related to character rather than activity, to a choice of values rather than a choice of jobs.

8   Materialism:
the Love of Money

Pierre Spoerri

DURING THE SIXTIES, if morality was mentioned, almost everyone thought in terms of sexual morality. But at the same time enormous pressures were going on in most Western countries in relation to consumerism, which raised just as many moral issues.

The possibilities of greed have never been higher because the availability of all sorts of consumer products is suddenly with us. The first crystal radio set appeared within the memory span of our oldest citizens; since then we have produced valve radios, transistor radios, colour television, video recorders, cable TV, satellite TV and satellite link-ups. We have witnessed the development of the telephone, then long distance calls, satellite-beamed international calls, portable phones and fax machines. This kind of rapidly escalating development has been repeated in field after field. One effect is an enormous incentive to earn more money to buy more of these things.

In the public eye, Switzerland has become one of the countries where the dark sides of materialism often overshadow the bright. As a Swiss, when travelling around continental Europe, I often hear the saying: 'No money, no Swiss'. And there is the definition of perpetual motion: a Swiss running after a Scot to whom he has lent a franc. A leading Swiss citizen admitted recently that 'the most sensitive nerve in a Swiss organism is the wallet.' When Frank Buchman spoke to a gathering in a mountain village close to Geneva, he said to the assembled Swiss after they had sung Luther's hymn 'A mighty fortress is our God': 'How many of you have actually been thinking, "A mighty fortress is my bank account"?'

Two key events in Swiss history involved money. At the

end of the fifteenth century, the Swiss cantons were attacked by the mighty Duke of Burgundy. In the first battle he lost his fortune, in the second his army and in the third his life. When the war came to an end, it was the distribution of the booty, amongst other issues, that almost led to a civil war between the cantons. A hermit, later made a saint – Nicholas of Flue – brought the delegates of the warring factions together at the last moment and succeeded in resolving the conflict.

But even after this intervention, since Swiss mountain valleys offered very little opportunity to make money, the young men of Switzerland continued to offer themselves as mercenaries to the various European powers. This worked quite well until 1515 when two armies – one organised by the King of France, the other by the Duke of Milan – met in a place called Marignano. Both armies consisted mainly of Swiss soldiers, and the losses were colossal. After this catastrophe, the leaders of the Swiss cantons met and decided that Switzerland would remain politically neutral for perpetuity. This decision remains valid today.

I grew up with two competing philosophies on money in our family. My father had a light-hearted and generous side to him. He took us children on walks, sometimes through gardens and parks that were theoretically closed to the public. When we had safely crossed the prohibited bits of territory, he would calculate the fine we had 'saved' and announce, 'Now, we're going to spend it!' My mother kept the accounts; when she died we found all the account-books from the day she got engaged in 1913 till the end of her life. Our view was that she turned over every five-franc coin several times in her hands before spending it. We never had much money in the house, but we never had to go hungry and were not prevented from going on outings or to cultural events with our friends.

Later, when our family became involved in the work of Moral Re-Armament and the creation and maintenance of its world conference centre in Caux,[1] my parents regularly gave quite large sums to this work. 'I just keep enough money in the bank in case one of us falls ill, and enough for my funeral,' my father used to say. Even as Vice-Chancellor of the university, he never owned a car and found it quite natural that we lived very simple lives. And during their latter years, my mother wholeheartedly supported father's generosity while still keeping an eye on the accounts. Amazingly enough, she succeeded in doing both.

When I married, two philosophies on money had again to be reconciled. I had inherited my mother's cautious approach, while my wife had grown up in situations where money lost its value very quickly due to inflation, so the best way to get value out of it was to spend it! I was reminded of this philosophy when I was confronted with unbelievable inflation rates during a visit to Poland in the autumn of 1989. For 50 Swiss francs, the cost of hiring a specialised Swiss worker for one hour, I was given the huge sum of 400,000 zloty, which corresponded to twice the monthly salary of a senior civil servant.

It seems obvious at the end of this century that a great deal of thinking is needed on an adequate philosophy of money to answer the present discrepancies between North and South on one hand, and to deal with the over-extended economies of the West and the economic collapse in Eastern Europe on the other. When in the autumn of 1989 the Berlin Wall crumbled and in the following spring the East Germans for the first time in a generation elected a free parliament, slogans of all kinds appeared on house-walls. They revealed that, while the emphasis of the struggle for much of the population was on freedom, for others it was on the fastest possible road to join the West, meaning the land of the strong German mark. A senior German official asked shortly before reunification, 'Are we now going to exchange one materialism for another – the theoretical materialism of the East for the practical materialism of the West?'

This is not a new question. The French writer and philosopher Alexis de Tocqueville wrote a century and a half ago, 'I seek to trace the novel features under which despotism may appear in the world. The first thing that strikes the observation is an innumerable multitude of men, all equal and alike, incessantly endeavouring to procure the petty and paltry pleasures with which they glut their lives. Each of them, living apart, is as a stranger to the fate of all the rest; his children and his private friends constitute to him the whole of mankind. As for the rest of his fellow citizens, he is close to them, but he does not see them; he touches them, but he does not feel them; he exists only in himself and for himself alone; and if his kindred still remain to him, he may be said at any rate to have lost his country.'[2]

Is this the picture of Western society which those who have fled from the East sometimes face, especially in the big Western cities? One attitude which must be particularly difficult for them to accept is the unquestioned belief of many Westerners who feel, 'We have won! Capitalism has been proved right!' Less difficult to accept is the attitude which is summarized in the title of the editorial in a major German weekly: 'The defeat of Marxism does not mean the triumph of capitalism'. The author ends with the thought: 'Is this (Western society) really the perfect society which will triumph for all time over Socialism?'[3]

During my lifetime there has been a change in political values. In the fifties, sixties and seventies Socialism, or at least Social Democracy, was in vogue in many parts of the world. Responsibility for the well-being of individuals rested more on society than on the individuals themselves. In recent years the predominant political thought in many nations has become more concerned with wealth creation than its distribution. The individual has again become solely responsible. But if many are thoughtful about how far the pendulum should swing, the state of the former Communist countries has seriously damaged the attractiveness of public ownership and socialist values.

John Stuart Mill, in his famous treatise *On Liberty*, wrote that 'all good things which exist are the fruits of originality' and that 'a State which dwarfs its men, in order that they may be more docile instruments in its hands even for beneficial purposes – will find that with small men no great thing can really be accomplished.'[4]

The great advantage of freedom is that it allows individuals to prosper, to use their talents and ambitions; and society benefits. Freedom itself imposes no limits. It does not demand that those who succeed share their gains with the losers; it does not require prosperous nations to limit their prosperity for the sake of poorer nations. Free societies will always remain full of inequalities and a cause of inequality, unless free peoples choose a deeper morality – the morality from which their freedom sprang.

The less control society imposes, which is the requirement of a free market economy, the greater the degree of self-control needed if society is to become just, fair and caring towards those who cannot compete. It must, of its own choice, put in place curbs on the unrestrained freedom of its markets if it is to safeguard the needs of its weaker members.

A senior American columnist who visited Eastern Europe regularly, wrote in 1989, 'The decisive question will not be what marginal help the West provides the Soviets and their allies to emerge from their distress. It will be how societies compare in decency and justice if they succeed in their aspirations.' The author then points out how, under Stalin, human envy was exploited to the utmost and adds, 'America's task ahead is to show that its system can prevent a similar exploitation of greed, that it doesn't automatically produce masses of human rejects along with its glittering material output. Capitalist democracy won the Cold War round. It will take a different kind of commitment to win the next.'[5] This is true not only for America but also for us in western Europe.

The individual capacity for greed, which our capitalist system to some extent uses, is the reason why our own personal attitudes to materialism are important, not just for each of us in our personal walk through life but for the societies in which we live. Any new approach to materialism must come, in our free society, from within ourselves.

9 Materialism: the Perspective of Possessions

John Lester

ST FRANCIS IS perhaps the best known and one of the most loved of Christian saints. His youth involved a search for pleasure and this world's goods, yet for the love of Christ he abandoned everything and lived as a poor man, begging for food, sharing all he had. He had so little, yet he had so much, for all that has been written about him reveals him as one of the finest of men. His inner life and his outward life merged. The one was neither distraction nor contradiction to the other. To his contemporaries, some of whom regarded him as completely mad but are now forgotten, he had nothing; but to countless fellow searchers through the centuries he has found everything that really matters.

St Francis is known as a poor man, a lover of poverty, but perhaps the most important characteristic to spring from his love of God was his obedience to him.

There may be nothing to stop anyone becoming wealthy, successful and also obedient to God, but a study of those most faithful to the inner journey shows that this obedience often required of them a separation from the goals of the world.

When I was about 20, I faced a new hurdle in the inner journey. Again I paced the hills wrestling with my conscience and something deep inside. I had come to accept God as real, but what did this mean in practice? I knew that I had given my life to him – apart from what I liked to think of as three 'small' things: marriage, career and money. Everything else was his. But I finally was faced with the knowledge that I could travel no further without looking at these three issues. What, I wondered, was I meant to do?

I decided, as a start, to give £200 to a charity. It had covered my expenses for some work done for it. I was not expected to pay the money back, but chose to be fully responsible for myself, and so I did. At that time £200 was a major part of what I had.

That simple act broke in me the tyranny of money. For the first time I realised that if my life is given to God then nothing, including money, belongs to me. This, I thought, ought to be serfdom – but I felt free. That freedom did not depend on having money or having no money; it depended on obedience. It came from a recognition first of all that my possessions belonged to him, and later that I belonged to him.

In attempting to pursue a life of obedience to God my wife and I found ourselves not long after our marriage in South India, in Madras. We had gone to prepare for the arrival of a musical revue with a cast of about 90 young Europeans, invited by Indians who felt it would be helpful to the area.

We were not earning. We had hardly any money, but we had a strong sense that we were where we should be. We were met at the airport by a New Zealand farmer and his wife. They had left their farm, and they too had no money. A Catholic priest had sold his watch, his only possession, to get them from Bombay to Madras, so strongly did he believe in what they were doing. An Indian businessman offered them and us his firm's guest house. So that was where we stayed.

There was no money for next day's food, though we were supposed to be finding lodging and food for 90 Europeans, in a city we did not know, as well as arranging all the theatrical details. There was a knock at the door. It was a friend, a university lecturer: 'I have been trying to get you a telephone. There is a ten-year waiting list, but they have promised to give one to you in view of what you are doing. But you must pay cash now. They need 400 rupees.'

A few minutes later, another knock at the door. A businessman was outside: 'My firm would like to take advertising in the programme you are preparing. Normally we pay after it is all over, but I had a feeling that you would be needing cash. Here it is.' It came to 400 rupees.

My wife went to see someone she thought might give accommodation. She was the friend of a friend, and my wife had never met her before. 'Could you have someone to stay?' she asked. It was not possible, but the woman offered to lend her bungalow. Her 'bungalow' turned out to be a very large empty house. Then a senior Catholic figure said that they had an ashram (a retreat house) that was not being used at that moment and we could take anything from it we wanted. With this we were able to furnish the house and install all the kitchen equipment we needed for meals.

On the first evening when the crowd arrived and were eating supper in the gardens of this big house, the university lecturer arrived with students from his and a neighbouring college. They joined us for supper. On their minds was the huge motor car manufacturing plant sited nearby which had been on strike-cum-lock-out for eight months. There are no social welfare benefits in India, and many of the workers' families were starving. The students were determined to bring together the warring factions – management, trades unions and government – but how?

First, the students came to the musical and saw that it portrayed the art of saying 'Sorry'. Inspired by this, they went to all the leaders involved, brought them to the show and then got them together. They listened to the students and finally to each other. In one week the strike was over, starving families began to eat again, prosperity to return and needed cars to roll off the production line. So many local people bought tickets for the show that by the time we were due to leave, not only were all the bills paid but we had enough for the fares to our next port of call.

There may be something in this story of value for a materialistic age. Those who turn away from the known path, who let go the normal financial securities – not because they are lazy or feckless, but out of a genuine desire to serve God – are in one sense poor, and yet may find themselves able to do things of a magnitude that bears no relation to what they possess and which many, even with resources, might not dare to do. In that sense they are rich, certainly in terms of adventure.

This approach is not a recipe for irresponsibility, for the belief that someone else should look after you or that you can depend on someone else's foresight or hard work or thrift. But it does mean that God has his ways of looking after those who are trying to be obedient, and if that obedience deprives them of the chance to earn money then their needs will still be met. I have had the experience both of living in this way and of earning money. I know that each is part of a whole. If I am earning, then the money I earn is still God's money to be used as he directs.

Altogether my wife and I spent three years in India. It was for us a different world. We sat one day on the cow-dung floor in the home of a villager with whom we had become friendly. His home was a one-room affair, erected from local materials. The floor was devoid of furniture. There was nothing in the home except a cooking fire and his family. Yet if we had asked him what it felt like to be poor he would not have known what we meant, for he did not regard himself as poor. Whenever we visited, he and his wife offered us a meal. If we could not stop, they offered us vegetables from their smallholding.

There are still many people in rural India who have not yet been afflicted with the 'consumer virus' which produces an insatiable appetite for more. Of course, within India, it is also quite easy to find plenty of people who have bad cases of the 'virus', who desire quite as much as their counterparts in the West, who know how to flaunt their wealth and who are oblivious to the poverty all around them. But India made us reassess values which up to then we had taken for granted.

I am grateful for the chance of knowing, even a little, what it is like to be without, for it gives compassion for the truly poor who have no means of getting out of their dilemmas. Yet I have never found it difficult either to mix with those who are well off. But so often the people with more can feel tempted to gain more still, to move from a small car to a big one, from a town house to an additional country house, from furniture to antique furniture, from holidays to foreign holidays, from a dinghy to a cruiser. They become the slave of their own desires. Possessions become an addiction – something we can all become prey to – and the spiritual path becomes less and less distinct, further and further away. Realism replaces idealism, cynicism replaces faith.

It is hard to keep the question of material prosperity in perspective. Our age has unleashed so much material progress, which rushes on at ever-expanding rates. We need oil, we need coal, we need nuclear energy because we want to have more and more things, to go to more and more places more and more often. There seem to be no limits.

Yet there are limits. There are the limits of a finite environment. For all the previous centuries when man has been around, the earth, the sea and our atmosphere have been a very efficient recycler. Trees, growing over the millennia, have become coal and oil. Nothing has been wasted. All our rubbish has been converted back into useful chemicals. Now, for the first time, the scale of man's activities is such that we are capable of overpowering the natural buffering and restoring capacity of nature. Not only are we capable of it, it is happening in many different ways.

It is only now that our material growth and knowledge have multiplied so fast. We have become the first generation able to benefit from the skills of all generations. But if we take all we can, we could leave a spoiled inheritance to our children and grandchildren. So there is a cost to materialism which we may not have to pay: it will be others yet unborn who pay the bill.

But not only them. For we also have to face the trauma of the developing world. So many, in Africa for example, had their freedoms curtailed through colonial conquest. When they finally gained independence, they became yoked to a world economy fuelled and controlled by growth in the developed world, from which their colonial masters had come. Because of their inability to control the price they are paid for the raw materials they provide and because of the huge burden of debt repayments on loans originally taken to enhance development, both development and growth have been stifled. They remain poor in spite of the increasing wealth of the Western world; to some extent they remain poor because of the increasing wealth of the richer nations. They are prisoners of a world economy in which they cannot compete on equal terms, with many millions suffering also from the ravages of both war and famine.

This is a moral dilemma of freedom which we cannot escape. Economic freedom in one part of the world is causing economic imprisonment in another. The answer to the self-interest harnessed by capitalism is not the bitter legacy of

Karl Marx. It is the message of St Francis, the decision to make moral and spiritual goals more important than material ones and to put the needs of others before our own.

10 The Pervasiveness of Permissiveness

John Lester

I ONCE DELIVERED a baby in a cubicle in a casualty department. The mother was a young teenage girl who had come to the hospital with undiagnosed abdominal pain. She had not found the courage to tell her own mother, who was outside, that she was pregnant. The baby's cry revealed the truth. I then had three patients to deal with. Recently I was treating a young man for an infection, but the real problem turned out to be early AIDS. A young girl came to see me who had been accepted for university, but I had to tell her that she was pregnant; she wanted an abortion.

It is impossible not to sympathise with the heartaches people face as a consequence of their own actions. I have always felt, however, that it would be wrong for me to condone an abortion or to take any part in such a process. I prefer to counsel mothers to accept their child. If they choose to see another doctor then that is their prerogative. Sometimes they go elsewhere; sometimes they accept counselling. I have in my mind a young child, the apple of her mother's eye, who would never have been born if the mother had done what she originally intended.

It seems to me that the pressures under which people live are greater now than they were even when I first qualified. Certainly the questions I have to ask are different: 'Have you run the risk of pregnancy?' 'How many partners do you have?' 'Have you had any homosexual encounters?' 'Have you ever taken drugs?'

Doctors have to deal with people and their problems where they are. It is our job to care, not to judge. But it is important also to understand what has happened in society and what is still happening.

Our Western civilisation was launched on Judeo-Christian

73

values, which enabled freedom to develop and flourish. Such freedom is based on the sovereignty of God and the premise that, although mankind has been given free will, there are nonetheless recognisable standards of right and wrong by which behaviour can be judged and according to which our laws should be framed.

With the Enlightenment, in the eighteenth century, another concept of freedom emerged; it was based on the sovereignty of man, a secular morality which implied a rejection of the sovereignty of God. It developed the right of individuals to make their own standards and in so doing discarded absolute values. Whilst it has encouraged the development of individual rights and initiatives, and been an important strand in our historical development, it has, through its antipathy towards absolute values, encouraged permissiveness, which so easily results in an abuse of freedom.

Those values in the West which had developed from 'revelation' and those liberal values which had developed from 'reason' came into conflict rather than developing in tandem – mainly, we would argue, because those who advocated reason had turned against belief in God, although religious people share some blame for not having always been open to truths coming from other sources.

Many people can recite the causes of the First World War and outline the rise and fall of Fascism or Communism, but fail to understand the struggle over values which has been taking place throughout this century, which relates directly to these two concepts of liberty.

There was a lie at the heart of Communism. Truth was made subservient to the will of the state; what the state decreed as true had to be accepted by all as true. Those who remained faithful to their belief that truth was an absolute value, not to be distorted or confused with falsehood, kept their integrity but faced imprisonment and death; we do not know how many perished, or were psychologically damaged or destroyed. Those who decided to pretend that falsehood was truth in order to keep their jobs, protect their families, preserve their lives, had to live with untruth in their souls. The lie at the heart of the state had to be maintained by the refusal to make an issue of it, thus producing a lie in millions of hearts.

But there is also untruth at the heart of our secular society: that God's laws are fictional, that there are therefore no fundamental moral values on which individual lives and the law can be based, that standards which challenge secular, permissive, values should therefore be opposed.

Under Communism, truth was what the state said it was. With permissiveness, truth is what the individual decides it is. Totalitarian societies force people away from God; permissive ones tempt them away.

In the eighteenth century, in Britain, the spiritual revival of the Wesley brothers began and was nurtured.[1] Because of it the secular values of the Enlightenment, spreading initially from France, could not gain much ground. The Wesleys were followed by others – Wilberforce and the Clapham Sect,[2] the Quakers and social reform,[3] Newman and the Oxford Movement.[4] Similar examples could be given from other countries. It was in their religion that many people, including those imprisoned by poverty and class injustice, found both meaning for their lives and an inner liberation.

Many have now forgotten just how this revival penetrated and how much of it we have lost in recent years. My grandfather, preaching as a Methodist minister in Birmingham, could be sure of a congregation of over a thousand working men and their families every Sunday. And it was the deep current of religious life and thought that kept moral standards of behaviour in place.

In 1914, many went into the First World War with a surge of idealism. That was to be effaced by the terrible trials of the trenches. At the beginning of that war Britain was a predominantly Christian country; she emerged with her faith badly mauled.

'What killed the idea of orderly, as opposed to anarchic, progress, was the sheer enormity of the acts perpetrated by civilised Europe over the past four years,' wrote Paul Johnson of that period. 'That there had been an unimaginable, unprecedented moral degeneration, no one who looked at the facts could doubt.'[5]

One result was that absolute standards of morality, began to be replaced by relative ones. The secular values spawned by the Enlightenment began to take hold even in those countries in which they had hitherto been resisted.

Just as it took a lessening of the hold of the Christian faith upon the imagination and life-style of millions of ordinary people to make this change in attitude possible, so when the changes in behaviour began to be generally accepted they made further inroads into our spiritual capital and hastened a decline in popular religion.

There has been through the century a stepwise decline that to some extent has an irresistible logic to it. Like a mountain walker on a steep slope moving down, it is hard to stop, more difficult to climb back, easiest to go on down. In the middle of the century it became more firmly established that human behaviour was a matter of opinion, that individuals must decide for themselves, that it did not matter what you did so long as no one got hurt. Britain began to question the merits of sexual continence. The sexual revolution was the natural starting-point for a permissive revolution which was to lead to many unexpected results.

The sexually active are in any generation mostly young. Our grandfathers went to church and believed in its teaching. They passed on to their children, our fathers, their code of conduct, but they failed to pass on their faith, battered as it had been by the turmoil of earlier years. Our fathers had little faith to pass on, yet they hoped to pass on their moral standards. But alas, separated from their roots, it was not possible to pass on the real reasons for such 'rules'.

The Christian reason for chastity is that obedience to God's will demands it; and much can be written about the gains for individuals, families and society that spring from it. The human, utilitarian, reason is that unwanted pregnancies or venereal diseases may result if it is not followed. The advent of the contraceptive pill and penicillin was to remove for this generation for the first time in history the human reasons for the standard – although not the religious reasons. The young, deprived of spiritual teaching, could not accept the religious reasons. The temptation for sexual experimentation was a powerful urge.

Presumably, since the beginning of time, men and women have been prey to sexual temptation. Promiscuous life-styles are not new. But not only have they been regarded most of the time by most people as wrong, it was also impossible for any individual to pursue sexual license without facing the practical consequences.

Contraception, coming at a time when so many were beginning to doubt the moral norms, was to change a great deal. Whilst it was never the cause of permissiveness, it made heterosexual activity safe and ushered in the permissive revolution.

With the contraceptive pill, the sexual act was separated in the minds of millions from the act of procreation. There was a veritable explosion in sexual relationships, the effects of which are only now beginning to become apparent. All through history, the act which initiates the creation of a new life had been linked with love and occurred normally within a stable, long-term family setup. This is still true for many couples. But the discovery of the Pill, in separating these functions, trivialised sex so that the balance between love and lust was tilted for many in the direction of lust.

This also altered many people's conception of human life. Life could now be prevented. The intention of the sexual act was no longer to create life but often involved actively preventing it. As sex became more mechanical so human life became less valued. Without this subtle, unrecognised effect, it is unlikely that we would have accepted the changes to the laws on abortion.

The pressure for readier abortion came for several reasons. In the first place, whilst it was expected and intended that the Pill would produce fewer unwanted pregnancies, there was such a dramatic increase in sexual activity that there were more unwanted pregnancies than before. Secondly, many were becoming pregnant who could least afford it, such as young teenagers. Thirdly, those who had seen the Pill as a means of liberating women and making them equal with men, recognised that without the opportunity to decide for themselves over whether to 'keep' a pregnancy, if one should arise in spite of precautions, then they were not as free as they thought. So the pressure mounted inexorably for abortion on demand. It was viewed merely as a late form of contraception or a remedy for failed contraception.

Just as the Pill was brought in originally for bona-fide

family planning reasons, so abortion was ostensibly brought
in to clear up the anomalies: to make it legal for doctors to
perform those abortions which many were already perform-
ing for specific medical reasons, when the mother's life was
threatened. But as with the Pill, the new attitude soon spread:
if it is legitimate to destroy life for specific reasons, why is it
not allowed whenever the mother wants it?

One of the fascinating footnotes on the history of our times
will be the way in which in 30 years gynaecologists have
changed their standpoint. When my father was in his prime as
a consultant obstetrician, almost no gynaecologist favoured
abortion, liked carrying it out, or was prepared to carry it out
save in very dire circumstances, or wanted the law making it
illegal altered.

Now the great majority carry it out routinely, seemingly
with few qualms, and have no desire to see the law altered in
the reverse direction. What has happened? Some would argue
that the gynaecologists have seen the light, they have been
won over. It is likely that some of them would say just that.
But it may not be the whole story.

In the first place, many who would otherwise be drawn to a
career in obstetrics now avoid the speciality because it
involves a procedure with which they cannot agree. Others
who, in spite of this, want to stay within the specialty and
fight for change or at least to preserve their right to practice as
they see fit, have come up against all sorts of difficulties in
gaining appointments. Other doctors who have abandoned
their original principles are unlikely to be keen to appoint a
colleague who does not fit in, who reminds them of their
previously held convictions, and who, in not doing his share
of abortions, involves them in extra work which is anyway
not congenial. Thus the specialty of gynaecology is more and
more being staffed by those who 'don't mind'.

But what of those who used to believe one thing and now
accept another? Many doctors, the first time they do an
abortion and often for many times subsequently, feel a surge
of revulsion. But human conscience is a strange thing. If any
of us go in the face of what we believe to be right and do it
often enough, it becomes easier and easier until we no longer

notice. This has happened to many doctors: what they used to find alien they can now do easily.

And so an abortion law, which was introduced to legalise abortion in certain limited circumstances, has become abortion on demand. The acceptance of this, the lessening of the hold of the 'sanctity', or sacredness, of life on society, has itself led further.

11 The Struggle for Values

John Lester

A SOCIETY WHICH abandons absolute standards of morality
may feel free but opens itself to much difficulty. There are no
more recognisable certainties, behaviour which society has
abhorred gradually becomes accepted, and no one seems able
to find a valid reason why a further step should not be taken.

One of the next to appear was, in certain circumstances,
the practice of infanticide. It seemed cruel to some to allow
handicapped babies to go on living. They were likely to be a
burden on the family and on the community and might not
themselves have a good standard of life. Initially, it was
argued that if a child had multiple faults, and if survival
required surgery, then it was surely reasonable to withhold
surgery if it was not possible to cure all the faults, on the
grounds that it was wrong to set right only some of them.
Utilitarian arguments had once more come to the fore.

Some babies are born with a blocked food pipe. Without
surgery, they die. A relatively high proportion of Down's
syndrome babies suffer from this defect. Some paediatricians
elected not to operate and thus to allow them to die. More
refined testing allowed certain abnormalities, such as Down's
syndrome, to be detected early, and such foetuses were
destroyed by abortion.

But then came the argument: if it is permissible, for
example, to destroy a foetus of up to 24 weeks of life*
because of Down's syndrome, and if babies with Down's
syndrome plus other abnormalities are allowed to die, why
not allow the destruction of such a mongol child, without any
other abnormalities – after birth – if the defect was not
noticed early enough to perform an abortion? A few
paediatricians thus began a practice in which they sedated
severely abnormal babies, who would otherwise have
survived, so that they would not cry, and then 'demand fed'

---

* Current British law

them – fed them only when they cried. Such babies quietly expire.

Since normal foetuses are now destroyed by abortion, and some abnormal babies are quietly allowed to die, will the time come when infanticide will be practised on normal babies if they are not wanted? It may seem horrific and implausible to some, but all the other steps which have been mentioned and which are now accepted by so many originally felt equally horrific and implausible.

It is not many years, for example, since the idea of research on embryos, for however valuable a reason, was deemed inhuman and unacceptable. But once it was considered possible to destroy foetuses because they are not wanted what possible exception could be made for embryos, particularly if they were to be used for useful reasons?

Euthanasia, in its turn, follows naturally from infanticide. Voluntary euthanasia is currently a major issue in some European countries and in some American states. It is only conceivable because of what has gone before it, and it is not a stopping point. There soon follows the argument for forced euthanasia for the senile or mentally severely abnormal who cannot judge for themselves whether they want to die and who are a burden on the state and on their families.

All these procedures deprive individuals – born or unborn – of their rights and freedoms, because they deprive them of life itself.

The permissive wave, which started with sexual behaviour and pressured society to opt for utilitarian arguments against absolute values, then worked its way into many other walks of life. I remember reading a leader in *The Times* during the sixties in which the writer argued that though we had given up sexual continence we remained as a nation honest and did not tolerate violence. Some years later another editorial commented that whilst we may not now be as honest as we were we still did not tolerate violence. Now violence is a fact with which we have to reckon.

Morality is indivisible. Suppose we start with the core of society: the family. If the permissive philosophy is accepted, then it is presumably acceptable for one or other parties to have extra-marital affairs. That is, some would argue, freedom. But that is only possible through a loss of real love in the marriage and – unless by agreement on both sides – through deception.

There is dishonesty in thousands of marriages before there is divorce. It was thus impossible to accept permissiveness in sexual matters and not condone dishonesty as well. If at the very heart of a nation, within the family, there is dishonesty, how can it be kept out of industry and politics and much else? For if a man or woman cannot be honest with the one they have loved most, how much less will they feel any obligation to be honest with someone who means much less?

Then comes the question of violence. Sex and violence often meet, for where perversions are indulged, violence takes on sexual connotations. Many, who do so indulge, find that they 'require' ever more extreme behaviour to satisfy their cravings. Permissiveness is the mother of violence. Many have argued that pornographic material has no effect on the behaviour of those who read it. I was never convinced of this argument and the less so when one of my friends, the mother of three children, was viciously stabbed to death by a man who was acting out what he had recently read.

The sad thing is not just that some now indulge in violence that should shock, it is that millions who do not practise violence themselves are no longer shocked or shamed by it. An experiment was performed in which a group of people were 'wired up' so that their heart rates, respiration rates, and blood pressure could be measured whilst they watched violent films. What emerged was that a level of violence which initially provoked major changes in these physiological norms soon produced no effect, and the level of violence had to be continuously raised to produce the same reaction.

The gradual withdrawal of absolute moral values from society has had two major effects. The first is that it has accelerated the flight from faith. It has made many feel that God is too far away to have any practical effect. The second is that it has led to an acceptance of all sorts of behaviour – dishonesty, casualness, insensitivity and violence – which would not have been tolerated before.

The flirtation with permissiveness, which Western countries have been trying, is an abuse of freedom which carries with it the potential destruction of freedom itself if we allow that flirtation to become a real long-term love affair. For where a people cannot practise self-control, which is the essence of freedom, the end result becomes imposed control which is the essence of totalitarianism.

The increasing acceptance of the permissive view of freedom to replace that based on religious values and the decline in those values cannot be tackled only by a fortress mentality. Yet it should be opposed as far as is possible because of the falsehood on which it is based and the damage which it does to people. Those who have grown up without guidelines, without God, and are having to find their own way are unlikely, however, to be touched by 'rules' which were not accepted fully by their parents and which now seem unwarranted attacks on their freedom.

There is a hunger in many for God. Those who choose to look in the Gospels will find an interesting paradox. Does Jesus advocate rules or not? In his Sermon on the Mount[1] Jesus' teaching on many subjects is recorded. He says, for example, 'You have heard how it was said, "You shall not commit adultery." But I say this to you, if a man looks at a woman lustfully, he has already committed adultery with her in his heart.'[2] Very straight talking. Is this a rule? At another point he said in answer to the question 'Which is the first of all the commandments?', 'This is the first: Listen, Israel, the Lord our God is the one, only Lord, and you must love the Lord your God with all your heart, with all your soul, with all your mind and with all your strength. The second is this: You must love your neighbour as yourself. There is no commandment greater than these.'[3] Does this suggest that there are no other rules?

I have seen people handle this paradox in two ways. The first is to make the 'rules' something which one tries to live by, out of a sense of rightness, by self-effort. The motive for this may be good and straightforward. I know plenty of people who have no belief in God but who do believe that such standards are what society needs in order to work properly, and that their part is to try to live themselves as they think others should. The motive may equally be fear or conformity. Self-effort does not produce a satisfying life.

The second approach comes from those who say that because all they need is to love God, they can do what they like. 'I will love God and live naturally.' This often implies self-indulgence of one sort or another.

So what is the reconciliation of these two approaches? If we do come to know God and love him and our neighbour, then we want to live in a way that pleases him, not because we have to but because we want to. This is something quite different. In that case we will choose to study the Sermon on the Mount and all Jesus' teaching. We want to apply it – out of love for him and our neighbour. It is not because we will gain anything from it, nor because we have to, but because we want to.

The point of moral standards is tied up in a mystery. To live them for their own sake through self-effort, and to want them because they belong to God and because we love God, are not the same thing.

The first is indeed an effort. I remember having to go to bed with an eye complaint and a bad back from the strain of trying to hold to a discipline which I felt was expected of me. The second is a gift, something utterly natural. God's standards become normal because he is in us. The more we accept the more he may ask, so that we may choose to live a discipline stricter than the 'rules' would have insisted – but by choice, by desire, and quite without dullness or imprisonment.

'Blessed are the pure in heart,' said Jesus: 'they shall see God.'[4] This is a wonderful verse which refers to much more than sexual behaviour. Nonetheless there are many who regard any form of purity as dull and regard self-indulgence in sexual matters as fun. But such self-indulgence gives only temporary, transient satisfaction. For a few minutes it feels great. And then come the consequences, a certain dullness and insensitivity, and practical results which may be long lasting. Purity, on the other hand, is a gift from God – and is the gift of himself. God and impurity are opposites. If we choose God then impurity is burned away. There is not room for both in the human heart at the same time.

What is recorded in St Matthew's Gospel is not a set of rules – it is the qualities of God which we can be given and learn to treasure. They are the qualities God chooses for us. But just because they are not rules, it does not mean that we can ignore them: we cannot have him without the qualities he brings.

It is necessary for those who already believe in God to hold to and teach his standards as they have understood them. But those who begin to know and love God are also led to his standards. God takes each one of us where we are and shows us the next step towards him. That process is a long one. But the wonderful thing is that no matter how slow we are on the road or how far we fall from God there is always a step we can take towards him.

A difference of approach is necessary in this age compared with one or two generations ago. At that time the challenge to moral standards was a means of bringing people to an awareness of God. People knew what was right even if they had turned away. When they made a start to live as they knew they should, very often God became real and then they began to want to live wholly his way. This still happens. But now, in an age which has lost its moral guideposts, it is more likely that the beginnings of a vision of God will be the means of then leading people to his standards.

The debate on Christian ethics and morals generates much heat, shrillness of arguments and lack of respect for differing views. Christianity was born in weakness. It will advance through humility, not through force. The heart of the Gospel is not about morals, important though they are. Christ will probably not be discovered through attempts to cajole people to live in a certain way. Yet the discovery of Christ does lead people to live differently.

I believe that moral standards have an absolute value. Such standards may be beyond us; they may only be possible to follow with God's presence and help. But just as they may be the means of demonstrating our love for God, and just as they may be the fruit of his love for us, so too they may also be the best for society. If we want a world which is just and in which all have an equal share, then it will not be possible without moral values. Whether it be AIDS, or war, or the acceptance of squalor, these arise because we do not live by absolute moral standards, not because we do.

The mystery remains for those who choose to find it. Imposed standards – the puritanical approach – can be a form of imprisonment, a means of imposing uniformity. But the experience of God, which includes moral standards – a gift to share, not something to impose – is a liberating and freeing experience and encourages true diversity. It involves a far profounder concept of freedom than the one from which permissiveness stems.

12 The Desire for Gratification

John Lester

IN THE LAST chapters the effect of a false philosphy of freedom on society has been stressed. It is now time to look at how this affects individuals.

I sometimes wonder if I am unusual and if others sail through life without any worries about whether certain things are right or wrong. But I suspect that more people have questions, at least early on in life, than admit to them.

I came to believe, as a young man, that purity was one of the qualities God wanted for me; that I needed in all my dealings to be faithful to the wife I might one day have. This does not mean I was not tempted, but that simple thought kept me away from entangling sexual encounters throughout my university career.

One morning I had an unexpected thought: 'You will marry Elizabeth McAll.' I hardly knew her and rarely saw her, but it was a very attractive thought. It was followed by a sense that the time was not now, that I was meant to do nothing but wait.

By the time I had qualified as a doctor and was working hard in hospital, far away from where she lived and becoming more and more ambitious to succeed, I began to feel that this thought, which I had once believed came from God, was of no consequence. Instead, I thought I would go about things in a more natural fashion. It was not long before my wandering eyes led me into fascination with a certain nurse. Soon my feelings were roused. But somewhere deep down, although I was rebelling, I also knew that in the long run I wanted God's plan for my life.

So I prayed that God would reveal what was right. Two days later I had a letter from the nurse saying that she did not want to have anything more to do with me. I felt deflated and angry, not so much with her but with God. For what I had wanted was his blessing, and I could not help perceiving this as his veto. Then came an insistent sense that he had asked me to live by his standards and I had disobeyed; that I must once more accept these standards, and that in following him, I had no rights to marriage or anything else. I accepted. Within a short time my original thought returned, 'One day you will marry Elizabeth McAll.'

It still seemed unlikely. But before long I was required, for other reasons, to move to somewhere close to where she was living. The whole thing worked out simply and naturally. We have been happily married ever since.

It has been one of the marking experiences of my life, for in it I have seen God's love for me. I was stupid, because I was disobedient to the profoundest vision I knew. I could so easily have made an irreversible mistake; but God protected me. He did not have to. His choice for me, furthermore, has been so perfect that it has helped me to trust him in other matters.

Having been brought up in a stricter environment than today's, I went through a phase of fearing all sexual activity. I then came to recognise that in its rightful place it is a gift from God, and to understand the difference between the avoidance of what is impure and the positive qualities which have been kept in the monastic rule: chastity, poverty and obedience.

There is nothing intrinsically impure about normal, natural married love. It is, indeed, a gift. Chastity does not mean abstaining from what is impure or self-indulgent, which we should all do, but choosing to deny oneself the gift of sex for the sake of a deeper love of God. It is the recognition by those called to live that way, that in seeking to be 'wholly other' there is a need to cut loose the hold that the body has on the spirit.

A minority have a calling to permanent chastity, yet it has importance for us all. So many now believe that the full expression of our sexual urges is a right and necessary to avoid the danger of repression. This needs to be exposed as one of the falsehoods of the permissive age: and a study of some of those who have chosen chastity reveals personalities of great sensitivity and care who have had an honoured part in the development of Western civilisation.

For every human being sex, the source of our existence, is a major drive. At one extreme, it can lead to indulgence and exploitation; at the other it can be a source of fear. In the wrong context it trivialises life, deadens the spirit and makes God seem distant. In the right context it is a wonderful gift and teaches us more of God. It can also be a gift we yield to God to bring us closer to him.

The permissive age has encouraged much more sexual gratification and experimentation and made self-denial seem abnormal. As a doctor I have learned not to be surprised or shocked by the life-styles of the patients who come to see me, yet I do often feel concern and some sadness, for so many begin by using their freedom to do what they please and end up being imprisoned by their own appetites. We talk of 'free love' but it is not free – there is a cost to it: often in medical terms through genito-urinary disease, unwanted pregnancies and abortion; in social terms through the failure of family life; and in spiritual terms since so many, in turning away from God's commandments, feel far from him and do not know how to be freed from their own imprisonment.

Jesus referred to the 'pure in heart'. Purity is a quality which is recognisable but hard to describe in words: to be free from self – self-concern, self-interest, self-gratification, self-satisfaction. In today's world it is a quality under threat because self-realisation is regarded as one of the major goals in life.

Those who gain even a fleeting sense of God's presence want to live in a way that allows that vision to remain; purity becomes a quality which is desired. In deciding to exercise their free will by choosing purity they accept limitations to their freedom of behaviour. Yet they discover a new inner liberty.

There are plenty of people who reject this thesis. That is everyone's own choice. It is written here for those who feel that they have yet to find the 'pearl of great price' and do not know where to look, who feel trapped. They should know that they do not need to remain trapped.

Of those who appear in the surgery some are of note because of the degree to which sex comes to dominate their lives: couples who demand so much of each other that they

become tired of one another; those who then seek excitement
in 'dangerous' liaisons that so often cause marriages to fail;
those who become so besotted that they allow all other
activities to be adversely affected – studies that fail,
opportunities missed. There are also those who seek
satisfaction in what used to be termed 'perversions'. Some
activities are still so regarded and consequently kept hidden.
Others are now being openly promoted as 'alternative
life-styles'. The most obvious is homosexuality, which is
important to consider since it is the focus of so much public
attention.

The rationale for society to change its attitude to
homosexuality is that it frees a minority from becoming
second class citizens required to keep their 'preferences'
secret, living to some extent in a ghetto. But the pressure for
change lies one step back: if we accept that sexual
gratification in heterosexual relationships is always acceptable, that it is a right and even a necessity, then it becomes
hypocritical to urge sexual continence on others who seek
satisfaction in other directions.

This, of course, leaves out the spiritual dimension. The
Christian, knowing his or her own weakness, ought not to
point a finger of guilt at one group of people; but nor does the
Christian community wish to condone something which has
been considered wrong since Biblical times, since condoning
it will encourage others into that temptation. It can take this
stand precisely because it does not consider sexual
gratification for any of us to be either a right or a necessity. In
speaking out against homosexual practice it is being entirely
consistent, not persecuting one particular group. Until
recently this was not just a religious perspective, but the
generally held view of society.

We then come to the question of whether homosexuality,
to remain with the same example, can be cured. There are
many who say that it cannot. There are many homosexuals
who have no wish to be cured or who do not admit that there
is anything to cure. There are some who admit to a
homosexual orientation and who find the strength not to
indulge in homosexual practices. It is a recognition that the
sin lies in the practice not the orientation; just as there are

many heterosexuals, who do not indulge in sexual activity because they do not believe in sex outside marriage. The world owes a great deal to those who have sublimated their sexual energy into constructive, creative purposes.

But there is a further possibility. A friend was troubled by strong homosexual urges, but no longer has them and is able to cherish a happy marriage, blessed with children. This may not be common but it does occur, in spite of the efforts of some to convince people that it does not. It is possible to break free; perhaps the most important thing is for the individual to really want to be different. In this case it was not the result of psychiatric intervention but a prayed-for gift from God. Jesus invited us to ask for such spiritual gifts, above all, for his kind of love.

Today's world knows a good deal about the realities of power, but it has to a large extent forgotten the power of God to transform the most intractable parts of our nature: to forgive, to wipe clean, to make new.

One of the saddest occurences of the last years has been the development of AIDS. It was discovered in the homosexual community on the west coast of America. It spread rapidly through that community and among drug users. It is present in large numbers in Africa and Asia, spreading there largely through heterosexual promiscuity.* No one knows where or how it began. We need to work for a cure; we need to care for those afflicted.

When America's 'most charismatic basketball star', Earvin 'Magic' Johnson, revealed in November, 1991, that he had the AIDS virus and broke off his sporting career from one day to the next, and in the same month the rock-singer Freddie Mercury died within hours of confirming that he was suffering from AIDS, public discussion about this disease suddenly moved from the academic to a rather more down-to-earth level.

---

* The WHO estimates 5-10 million people are currently infected with the HIV virus and that globally one million people have AIDS. By the year 2000, 40 million people will be infected with the virus and 20 million will have AIDS. 90% of all these people will be found in Africa and Asia.[1]

In a long article, 'Magic' Johnson said, 'The way I chose to deal with HIV infection was to go public... I am certain that I was infected by having unprotected sex with a woman who has the virus. The problem is that I can't pinpoint the time, the place or the woman. It's a matter of numbers. Before I was married, I truly lived the bachelor's life. As I travelled around, I was never at a loss for female companionship... I was the one most NBA players looked up to when it came to women. I lived the kind of social life that most guys in the League wanted to lead. Now I'm pleading for every athlete and entertainer who has also been "out there" to get tested and, from now on, to practise safer sex... I've never been the kind of athlete who wears his religion like a shield, though I've been strong in my faith since childhood. That faith allowed me to accept the HIV infection when part of me was asking, "Why me?" '[2] He was courageous to come out openly with his tragic situation. But the link between promiscuity and AIDS is not made; he seems to think that 'safe sex' and the readiness to be tested will deal with the spread of the disease while allowing promiscuity to continue unabated. He has, since then, had second thoughts and has been reported as saying 'abstinence is God's way for young people'.[3]

A leader writer in *The Sunday Times*, commenting on the death of Freddie Mercury draws some basic conclusions: 'It is better to be sexually repressed than to be dying of AIDS. Indeed, a degree of sexual repression is obviously an absolute good. Without it there would be no culture ... The young people who are dying of AIDS are the victims of a bizarre assertion of nature's malevolence of a kind that most people thought our science and technology had made impossible. They are a mirror that reflects, for once, an unarguable reality.'[4]

I cannot agree with those who see in the emergence of this disease the judgement of God. What does seem true is this: if we had chosen to follow the teaching which came from Moses, Jesus and the founders of the other great religions, then we would have been protected from this particular catastrophe. To me, it reflects therefore not the judgement of God but the foolishness of man who chose not to heed God's instructions.

The secular view is that there is no such thing as sin and that we need to free ourselves from a feeling of guilt and the fear of retribution. The spiritual view is that sin exists and that God can free us from it. The first says that there is no 'disease', the second that there is a cure. Each person has to decide which philosophy is true.

13   The Bondage of Addiction

John Lester

WHEN I WAS working in the casualty department of a large general hospital, a man was brought in suffering from severe abdominal pain. I asked him what happened. He replied that he had been hugged by a bear. This seemed highly unlikely in the middle of Birmingham. But he told me that he was a zoo-keeper. He was taking the bear by truck from London to Manchester zoo and he had stopped to feed it in Birmingham. When he opened the cage some children screamed, frightening the bear which turned on him and hugged him.

He then told me that he was fortunate to know that there is a nerve under the chin of a bear, very similar to the 'funny-bone' in humans, which if squeezed will cause the bear to let go. This is what happened, but not before he had sustained serious injury.

As I examined him I noticed an old scar on his abdomen. He told me that it was the result of a kick from a giraffe. We admitted him, gave him Pethidine to relieve the pain, and monitored his condition. After some hours we became suspicious. When he needed more Pethidine we gave him saline in its place. Within an hour he had disappeared.

That weekend a nurse came from a hospital thirty miles away to a staff party. 'We have just had a most interesting patient,' she began, 'he was hugged by a bear...'

He was a Pethidine addict who managed with this story to gain not only his daily fix of Pethidine but free board and lodging as well. It was all, of course, a pack of lies, but a good experience for me for it was the first time I had come into contact with a drug addict. Since then I have listened to a number of stories, plausible and implausible but none as florid as this one.

Addiction is yet one more way in which self-gratification can lead to imprisonment of the body and the soul. There are many who go through life without coming into contact with serious addiction, but for many families, one or more of whose members are touched by it, it is a harrowing cause of deep suffering.

Whilst we have been contrasting some of the difficulties which face West and East, addiction – in the form of alcoholism, smoking and drugs – is a problem which is common to both.

There are many who enjoy alcohol without becoming alcoholics. But the degradation of those who are so addicted is part of the terrible waste of potentially useful lives.*

I had in the surgery a man who needed to talk. He had been an alcoholic but had succeeded in kicking the habit. Now his wife was afflicted in the same way but was denying it as so many alcoholics do. He was desperate. He recognised the signs 'I have been to hell and just managed to come back and I can't bear the thought of my wife going the same way.'

I talked, when at medical school, with someone who was senior to me and who always looked very tough and self-assured. He suddenly opened up and said, 'I am a lapsed Catholic and I drink too much.' A year or two later I had a card from him – he was serving as a doctor in an African mission hospital. It taught me never to judge from appearances and to recognise that people do not always stay the same.

Another fellow student was very fond of cigarettes. He became a professor of pathology. He told me recently that as a pathologist he had to teach students about the dangers of smoking, but he had reached the point where he could not complete his tutorials without lighting up. This convinced him that he had to stop which, with great difficulty, he did. But after some months he thought he could manage the occasional cigarette. After the first one an intense craving for nicotine returned and he had to go through the whole process of giving up again. Since then he has never touched another. 'I am like an alcoholic as far as cigarettes are concerned. I have to follow the same regime – "not one drop".'

---

* In the United States, for example, in 1990 there were 10 million alcoholics. The cost of alcohol abuse was estimated at 136 billion dollars. It claimed 65,000 lives, 22,000 on the roads.[1]

His tutorials will have carried the statistics of smoking, the sad wastage of lives, the additional medical care required, the cost each year to the nation's coffers.* There are some who still regard nicotine as a minor addiction. Yet many are severely hooked by it.†

I had a patient who had developed severe arterial disease through smoking. He was in imminent danger of requiring his right arm to be amputated if he did not stop. But he seemed content to use his already damaged arm to lift cigarettes to his mouth rather than stop smoking, which he had decided he could not do. It is one of the less acceptable facets of capitalism that now that smoking in the Western world has peaked because of the recognition of the medical dangers – but not, sadly, among young women in most European countries – the tobaccco companies have begun to push for increased sales in the less developed countries of Africa and Asia.**

In the surgery I have tried to help people with different habits, indulgences and addictions. I have noticed that similar points emerge from many people. There is denial as with the alcoholic, 'Doctor, you've got it wrong, this is not my problem.' There is self-deception, 'Oh yes, I could give it up any time I wanted to.' Then there is self-justification: 'I am afraid I have a very weak will.' This usually means a very strong will and the intention not to stop.

Then there is the 'try and' brigade: 'Doctor, I am going to try and stop.' This means, 'I know I should stop and I would like to but I am not prepared for the pain involved.'

Finally, there are those, like my pathologist friend, who say, 'I have decided.' Whatever methods they use, these people will succeed.

---

* The scale of the problem can be measured by the fact that there are 431,000 deaths in the European Community annually from smoking related illnesses.[2]
† According to the United States Surgeon General giving up tobacco is as hard as giving up heroin.[3]
** Some suggest that these advertising campaigns make little difference. The Norwegian experience suggests otherwise. Among 13-15 year olds there smoking fell from 17% in 1975, when a ban on advertising was introduced, to 10% in 1990.[4]

There are different levels of addiction, some psychological and some physical. They are experienced at their worst by those caught in the web of serious drug abuse.

This is a problem which has grown enormously in Western countries in the last 30 years. Before then it was uncommon here. That so many are already dependent on nicotine or alcohol weakens societies' case against drugs. The more permissive society has become, the further it has come from the Christian concept of the body 'as the temple of the Holy Spirit'; if people rule nothing out as being 'forbidden', they become ready to experiment in a fruitless and harmful search for meaning and excitement. Our vulnerability is a sign of our moral bankruptcy. Thirty years ago the Colombian drug barons would not have amassed such fortunes, because there was a general revulsion against drugs.

Fiona Rafferty wrote in *The Sunday Times*[5] about the amphetamine derivative 'Ecstasy',* supposedly the latest and 'perfect' party drug, which many have thought was relatively safe. It is to the nineties what cocaine was to the eighties. Half a million are now estimated to take it regularly. Thirteen people have died from it. She quoted a 28-year-old accountant. 'When I first took it in 1987 the feeling was amazing. It left you floating around in what appeared to be a wonderful world of love and peace. That's why it's so morally wrong, because one tiny pill can give you a feeling 1,000 times better than anything else can in life.

'Ecstasy in effect devalues everything from your achievements to your relationships, because all experience pales into insignificance after you've experienced the ultimate in bliss. I wasted an entire year of my life floating around in this wonderful world. I didn't notice at first that I was losing all my motivation and becoming paranoid. While you're on it, everything seems so real and positive, yet it lets you down very slowly. You sort of blend back into reality and don't like reality any more, because you think you've experienced a better reality.

---

* Methylene Dioxymethylamphetamine. One Ecstasy haul in Sheerness, Kent in November 1991 consisted of 1.2 million tablets with a street value of £24 million.

'It's not advisable to take it – not even once – because it doesn't stop at once. I know from experience that it can and does change your entire perspective, but not for the better.'

The drug problem will not go away. The amount of money to be made makes it a difficult problem to solve. The use of the law, the vigilance of the police and customs officials, and international cooperation are essential to safeguard the vulnerable. But they are not enough. Without a return to objective values, to the sacred which holds the abuse of the body to be an offence against God, those who are tempted will not have the strength to resist. We can feel compassion for them because we know that we can all be tempted towards addiction of one form or another.

Drug-taking offers the cruellest proof that the pursuit of liberty separated from morality leads not to greater liberty but to imprisonment.

But even with those who fall furthest it is essential to hold out the hope that cure is possible. I know someone whose life was almost destroyed by drugs. He was searching for meaning, had experimented and become trapped. He did not find real meaning in drugs, only the end of his health and sanity. In his despair he prayed for deliverance to the God whom he had never known. In spite of the fact that he was at the very bottom, he felt the presence of God and was enabled to stop taking drugs from that moment. His life has taken several years to put together again, to mend and to heal. But now he is well and free from his previous habits. He has found real meaning in the faith that has been revealed to him, and so the need for drugs has gone.

In the debate on inner freedom the important point is not to prove that some are free and some are imprisoned; it is to recognise that those who are imprisoned can become free.

14   Focus on the Family

John Lester and Pierre Spoerri

AS MORAL STANDARDS have lost their 'permanence' in the public mind, because of the general acceptance of relative values, so the argument that certain relationships need not be considered any longer as permanent has gained ground. The heart of the moral struggle in society has moved from values to relationships. Marriage and the family have taken centre stage.

Those who know the joys of a happy marriage, as we are both fortunate to do, realise what a precious gift it is and would not swap it for anything else. Some find it elusive. For those who have not known it, the commitment involved can appear daunting.

At the moment of taking marriage vows, each partner voluntarily relinquishes some degree of freedom. Yet it never feels like that if love endures. Two people become one and the things which one partner can no longer do, for love of the other, are not sought. Love, far from curtailing freedom, in reality preserves it.

Many young people in Europe, however, have to cross rough waters before they finally reach the not-so-safe haven of marriage. It is widely accepted for couples to live together before they are married. Tensions between parents are often offered as an explanation for not wanting to enter into a permanent relationship without an initial trial period.

Once the decision to marry is reached, however, the marriages are often more stable than those that are the result of sudden youthful impulses. Pierre and his wife, for instance, were profoundly moved by the wedding service of a couple who had reached the decision to marry only after long years of hesitation. Instead of wedding presents, they asked for contributions for a conference centre in India where they had found a new basis for their shared faith. Just because tradition and custom do not play such a central part in this generation, the quality of the relationships freely entered into should not be underestimated.

The crisis in family life was under discussion in Russia, even while the officially atheistic Soviet Union still existed. A social scientist from the Soviet Academy of Sciences, speaking at a Family Congress in Bonn during the spring of 1989, deplored the fact that the divorce rate in the Soviet Union came second after the United States and was much higher than in West Germany. Young families are responsible for a large proportion of divorces there, so the problem of family stability is essentially a youth problem. According to the speaker, the policy of *perestroika* brought about a change in priorities that improved the chances of the family. 'The ever-increasing *glasnost* and tolerance of other opinions', he said, 'have removed the reasons for "double-think", as George Orwell put it. If we apply it to the period of stagnation, we could speak of "triple-think" when people said one thing, did another and thought a third. As a result, the traditional contradictions between fathers and children can now be settled in a democratic way free of lies and cover-up.'

The candid admission by a Soviet scientist of the needs of his society was astonishing at the time: so was his search for fundamental answers. He stated that to restore the family, some accepted basic values were necessary, and that he was asking himself whether the Ten Commandments recorded in the Old Testament[1] could play that role. He then asked his Western counterparts to take part in a study of the role of the Ten Commandments in Western and Eastern society.

For all of us family life is a challenge. The fact that it is now under threat, with some suggesting that the ideal cannot be sustained and so should not be required, makes the struggles of us all that much more important. The willingness to be open about feelings and things that go wrong, not only with one's partner but also with children, as they grow and understand more, is not easy but reinforces both love and trust within the family. It allows the relationships between the family members to grow.

All parents remember the moment when their first child was born, the sudden overwhelming surge of affection, protection, and belonging which is repeated with every succeeding child and has been experienced by numberless generations. As children begin to grow there is the new experience for the parent of love reciprocated, the inexpressible feeling of joy when they first run towards you and fling their arms round you. As children grow towards adulthood, they need to learn independence. Love cannot be a clinging thing which restricts their freedom. Children have in love to be given their freedom; the ability to find their own way. Parents can do their best to inculcate their values, but each generation has to be allowed to discover for itself, and parents have to learn on the job.

Without some basic values, which the Soviet scientist was looking for, it is less easy for any family to sustain itself through the tribulations of life. For children the need for stability and the concept of permanence are paramount, principally for their emotional development and maturity, but also to help them understand something of the permanence and reliability of God. Family life at its best is the natural setting in which many people through the ages have learned something of God's love for them. In Christian teaching, and that of other religions also, marriage carries within it the sacred and is associated with permanence.

Those who accept this, and who live accordingly, are given additional resources to help to make marriage work. In the first place the very concept of permanence, the acceptance that divorce is not an option, makes people work harder at marriage. If it goes sour there is a strong motive for working to restore it. In addition, the values which faith brings into a marriage provide the means for putting things right.

These values include the concept that love is not only a feeling but also a decision: that we can decide to care for someone always and to work at it. They also include the belief that the resolution of most disagreements lies in being able to say sorry and being able to forgive hurts and wrongs – to toss them into 'the sea of forgetfulness'. Finally, there is the knowledge that none of us needs to stay the same, that we can become different: that God himself can intervene and that none of us is unchangeable or beyond redemption.

We both know couples, separated or on the point of

separation whose marriages have been remade through honesty and forgiveness; and above all by the willingness to turn to God together and listen to him.[2] We know, too, individuals whose marriages have irretrievably broken down, sometimes for reasons beyond their control, who have found peace through forgiveness.

Sadly, we know others whose marriages have broken down with great bitterness and recrimination, and long-term consequences for all concerned. The ending of a marriage can have profound repercussions. John had a patient whose husband suffered a major heart attack on the day she told him that she was leaving him. The *British Medical Journal* reported that those who divorce are at greater risk of premature death than married people. This has been shown for every country with accurate health statistics for all ages and both sexes. The impact on the health of children is especially severe, with a higher risk of ill health from the time of parental separation until adult life.[3]

It is possible to feel great sympathy for those whose marriages, despite the best intentions, finally come to grief, and yet to believe that breakdown should never be accepted as a normal state of affairs.

One couple, whom we both know, have just celebrated their golden wedding. In reflecting on 50 years of marriage, the wife admitted that even on her wedding day on the way from the church to the reception, while holding the hand of her husband she had thought, 'Suppose it doesn't work?' The thought was hardly into her mind before another one, much more definite, took its place, 'Change is always possible.' Today that thought might be taken to mean, 'You can swap partners any time you like.' For her it meant that neither of them would need to go on being or doing whatever it was that was making life difficult for the other.

'Like some other couples we have met,' she continued, 'we have had our moments. We each have our strongly held ideas and can be annoying and hurtful to each other. My tongue, particularly, doesn't want to stop wagging till it's had the last word. This is when the thought, "Change is always possible", has proved so helpful. It causes me to turn to God and ask, "What's wrong with *me*?" The answer is nearly always immediate and more like a light being switched on than a spoken word. It has sometimes been friends who have done this for me by some remark they have let drop. The result has been a different picture of the situation, an understanding objectivity, a strong desire not to make the same mistake again and a dropping of my "right" to feel hurt, annoyed or resentful. As the years go by, this process is needed less often and takes up far less time. The light seems permanently on now, but each hurdle jumped over in this way seems to have landed us on a slightly higher and increasingly warm plateau of closeness. We don't even have to say we're sorry, we know it and we often marvel at the number of times we come out with exactly the same thoughts at the same instant.'

Her daughter remembers one of those 'moments', when she was still a child and things were not going well. She was afraid for a while that her parents would split up, and can still recall the agony of spirit she went through, the sense of being torn in two. Happily, family unity was eventually restored. When we celebrate the wedding anniversaries of those who have been married for a long time, we are not so much giving thanks for those who have had an easier ride than the rest of us but for those who chose permanence and were prepared to overcome the difficulties together.

Some marriages will be easier than others, but even the happiest marriages offer scope for growth. In any marriage a certain staleness can arise. A relationship which started so warmly can grow gradually cooler. At some periods in life a couple may naturally be doing exciting things together. At other times the 'doing' side of life becomes routine and the relationship depends on the quality of 'being' together. John and his wife endured one such 'flat' period which troubled them. When they finally asked God what to do, new steps on the hidden inner journey towards him were revealed which proved to be real adventures which allowed their relationship to blossom again. It seems that no relationship can grow unless it is worked at. Without growth there tends to be shrinkage. In growth lies the secret of continuance.

If we can accept change for ourselves within the family circle, then this change will move beyond the family to transform society, and through our children will affect the future. If we cannot make marriage and the family work, then what hope is there for less significant relationships?

When two people marry it is not just a bond between them that is formed, it is a bond between two whole families, often known in Asian society as the extended family, and is part of the ongoing structure of society. Any division within the family causes disintegration within the hearts of many people. It damages not just one couple but the whole family. This includes those who are single and those without children of their own, aunts, uncles, cousins, each of whom have their own unique part to play in the growth of the family. It is worth recognising that at a time when the marriage relationship is under scrutiny, so too the role and worth of those who are single is also being played down. Both the commitment of marriage and the discipline of the single life are at variance with today's uncommitted world, which regards living for oneself as normal and living for others as abnormal. This attitude, which results in so many older people in the West living by themselves, is so hard for the Asian communities, for whom the extended family is still so real, to understand

In the past a limited number of marriages broke down. This was in part, certainly throughout Europe, the result of an adherence to the Christian concept of marriage, and to the law as it stood, which had been informed by Christian values and which made divorce difficult. It also reflected an attitude to pain. Pain, both emotional and physical, was regarded as a normal part of life to be borne with fortitude. Marriages in which love died still remained intact. Nowadays, many assume that they should be without pain and regard it as a reason for avoiding or breaking promises.

This relates closely to the two views of freedom which lie behind this analysis of values and relationships. In the traditional view, based on the sovereignty of God, freedom carried with it responsibilities. A man and a woman, in marriage, each have responsibility for the other, for their children and their wider family which keeps them together, even through pain. Today many have accepted the secular view of freedom which has emphasised rights rather than respon-sibilities, in this case the right of the individual to separate or divorce if pain intervenes.

There are millions of people who are happily married, or who belong to happy families, who will defend the institution of marriage vigorously but for whom the spiritual dimension has neither interest nor significance. The family, however, seems to be under attack for the same reason as moral standards were earlier – the determination by some to remove God's 'monopoly' on human values and relationships. To the secular mind it is galling that religion, so largely abandoned, should still carry such weight in questions of marriage and the family. This fuels the desire to separate all relationships between people from religious teaching and place them only in the context of individual choice.

The argument for marriage, that it provides the most secure framework for everyone involved and the best environment for raising children, is a strong one. Few challenge the belief that married life is the ideal setting for bringing up children. It is not realistic either to challenge the whole concept of the family. It is, however, attacked tangentially: by demonstrating the fallibility of many married relationships; by showing that other types of relationship, such as cohabiting, can be secure, loving and successful; and by seeking to change the law to make divorce ever easier.

The argument for alternative life-styles rests on the individual's right to choose. Two people marrying for life remains acceptable. Suppose others wish to marry only for as long as love shall last, then their relationship should be given equal value. If two people wish to live together but have no formal tie, or if two of the same sex wish to live together in a 'married' relationship, then that too must be accepted. People must decide for themselves, society should make no judgements, and every person's view should carry equal weight. Authority thus passes from God and his absolute values to individuals and their relative values.

This argument has impacted society both because it seems to legitimise selfishness and because it has involved a continuing battle to change the law, so that both marriage and divorce are made easy and free of any obstacles, so that tax and inheritance laws are amended to ensure that those who only cohabit are not disadvantaged, and so that children born out of wedlock or even adopted by homosexual 'parents' can have the same rights as children born in marriage. Society recognises this as being fair on the children, but is caught in a cleft stick since we can also see that it is pursued as a device to legitimise alternative life-styles.

All this certainly ensures that society recognises people's rights, but does little for responsibilities. Family life becomes that much more precarious, because people are encouraged to take the easy way out when things are difficult. It has encouraged and condoned the huge increase in divided families with all the consequent effects on the security and emotional maturity of children, on the values and judgements which they will later pass on to their children, on society itself and on the economy. It is a philosophy which encourages fragmentation.

Many try to convince themselves, and others, that this fragmentation will be relatively painless. Those who consult a doctor because of marriage breakdown reveal the falsehood of this hope. They come with depression, insecurity and inferiority, or anger and self-righteousness, bitterness, grief and all the symptoms of bereavement. Statistics are one thing. When marriage failure happens to those you love, the sadness and pain which lie behind each statistic are revealed. The cost of the pursuit of a secular view of freedom has already been too high.

Fortunately, for all the arguments for less committed relationships that are being made, most people still choose the road of marriage and believe in faithfulness. In family life as it is experienced by many, love grows. The family deserves our protection, for it remains the fundamental unit for the future of all our societies.

15   Can we be Free of our Reactions?

Pierre Spoerri

ALL RELATIONSHIPS are based on how we react to and interact with each other. It is perfectly normal to react to the people and things around us. Reaction, or response, is part of the essence of life. Once we no longer react, we are dead, if not physically then at least emotionally.

From the moment of birth, a child's nervous system develops as a reaction to the stimuli of his surroundings. When first the mother, then other influences, stimulate the senses, nerve cells develop and establish communicating links with each other. The links between the ten billion nerve cells in one human being can become so dense that strung together they would extend to the moon and back. But if the stimuli during the first years of a child's existence are poor, the development of the whole organism slows down; the connections themselves are less well developed.

Reaction remains only in part a conscious process, even in adulthood. It is estimated that on average, 600,000 bits of information reach the human brain every second. Four-fifths of these come through the eyes. But from this huge amount of information, only ten to 20 bits reach the human consciousness, and only one is registered in the long-term memory. This long-term memory is estimated to have a capacity of 400 million bits. If we had to react consciously to every impulse coming from the outside, our minds would become completely clogged up; but there is an astonishing ability in the brain to sort out what information has to be moved into our consciousness and what information can be dealt with by the autonomic nervous system.[1]

While for a human organism, conscious and unconscious reaction is an obvious and constant necessity, on the level of social and international relations the word can take on a different meaning. In human relations, reactions are not automatic but subject to our emotional and social responses. If one side asks a question, and the other answers, this can be considered a genuine and legitimate response. But in the political field, for instance, 'reaction' has become a purely negative term. If someone says that there is a policy of reaction, what is meant is that it has no creative aspect and is simply a means of hitting back. In that sense, reaction in politics has become almost the norm. For decades, East-West relations, for instance, or the relationship between the West and the Muslim world, followed exactly this kind of predictable pattern.

This is not the place to consider in detail the role of pressure groups and the media in predicting, and anticipating or even demanding such a pattern of reaction and counter-reaction. But the leaders of nations seem constantly pushed by these forces in one direction or the other. They rarely seem free to break out of this kind of decision-making under pressure. And when they do it, they often find themselves confronted with a barrage of criticism and misunderstanding. It is refreshing to find that some of them still succeed in finding the right balance between inner conviction, which amounts sometimes to a kind of pressure also, and outer pressure.

The family is often the smallest unit in the reaction/counter-reaction game and for Westerners the motor car is often one of the classic settings where it can be best observed. An incident on a German autobahn comes to mind. I was sure that there was enough petrol to get home. My wife kept insisting on another refuelling stop. The more she insisted, the more I resisted. I kept on driving and, of course, thirty miles from home the engine suddenly started to cough and then stalled. In itself, the incident was ridiculously small. But the loss of pride went so deep that even days afterwards, when my wife had long forgotten the whole thing, I was still licking my wounds.

Two things determine the further development of such a 'crisis': the present state of the relationship between the two people involved, and the past history of that relationship. I react differently when I am challenged or corrected by a small child, a stranger, a senior person I respect or fear, a younger colleague, my wife or my mother-in-law. The reaction to a person close to me is often much more strong, because I am reacting not just to the specific event but to the whole history of the relationship.

The Swiss author Max Frisch illustrates in his book *Montauk* one aspect of such a relationship when he writes of '... my touchiness when, not having accused myself, I am finally handed out admonitions in private. A pathological touchiness: the reverse side of self-accusation, which is itself a reverse side of self-righteousness. As if it were not for others to judge what weaknesses I have, what errors I make.'

Frisch illustrates this with the story of a newly acquainted man and woman driving out together from New York to Long Island. The man – who is driving – gets into the wrong lane on the highway. ' "Max, you are wrong," says the strange young woman, and he takes it like any natural person, any healthy, reasonable person. That is a relief to me, for I had not really thought him capable of it ... He does not feel it as a rebuke. He realises that he should be taking the left-hand lane, and he simply does so, without saying sorry and then relapsing into a vexed silence. He sees it as a little act of helpfulness, not as a reproach.'[2]

The human memory resembles a computer. Short-term memories are registered in the form of electrical currents, long-term memories as chemical compounds. The details of this process are not fully known; the general outline is understood, but we do not yet know how our brain decides what memory to recall at any given moment.

It is clear that much of this 'recollection' is not in our power to control. In a conversation with a couple whom I know well, when the name of a certain city and some elements of past history were mentioned the wife started to breathe heavily, blushed and was unable to say a single word more. As this happened in the course of a dinner-party and the general atmosphere had been cheerful and relaxed up to that point, the subject of the conversation was quickly changed. Amazingly enough, soon the lady was her normal self again.

The accumulation of previous incidents that have never

come to the surface and therefore have never been cured, means that in a crisis there is an almost automatic explosion of feelings or an equally automatic freezing of all communication with the outside. Most of us have heard in school about the conditioned reflexes of the dogs in the experiments of the Russian scientist Pavlov. When he tried to apply the same principles to human beings – to make 'brainwashing' a reality – he fortunately failed. Human reactions are not as automatic and unconscious as the conditioned reflexes in animals, but some of them have similar characteristics.

There is a different depth and quality to a reaction according to its origin and intensity. First, there is the immediate, impulsive reaction, such as happens a hundred times a day. Many reactions of this type do not even enter the short-term memory. And as in a computer, their effect can in most cases be erased relatively easily and quickly. It usually takes a simple recognition of having made a mistake, or having used the wrong word, to close the incident.

We often realise ourselves when the second level of reaction is reached – when we suddenly feel that the intensity of the reaction is out of proportion to the size and importance of the incident that has provoked it. Under normal circumstances, when there is no crisis, all is well. But then suddenly there is an almighty blow-up. When a relationship has reached the stage where conscious and unconscious feelings threaten to escalate every time there is a disagreement, there is a choice between various courses to follow.

One way is to tackle the other person head-on and to explain to him/her in no uncertain terms where he/she has gone off the rails and needs to change his/her ways. The 'confrontational method' produces results of one kind or another, but with people with whom one has to continue to live at close quarters, it very rarely succeeds. The trouble is that these people know us too well and have heard all our arguments before!

The second method is one that the world often associates with 'humble' Christians. It consists in trying to defuse a situation by taking the whole blame on oneself. For a while, such a method may create a superficially better atmosphere, but as the root causes of the reactions are not looked into, it rarely produces a permanent solution.

Another unsuccessful method grows out of the deeply human desire not to accept as fact things we do not want to face. So we pretend that we are not reacting at all and push our feelings down. If we do this too often, we are no longer conscious of feeling anything. But sooner or later, the unconscious feelings trigger off an explosion anyway. So it may be better to let one's feelings out.

If these processes, which happen in and around each one of us every day, are not looked at realistically again and again, we may find ourselves locked in a relationship where reaction has become practically second nature. Such 'frozen relationships' are often found in families, most frequently amongst the older members. But the younger generation are not exempt. During adolescence especially, a constant state of reaction is common. Many fathers and sons are locked in tight, exclusive, reactionary relationships; mothers and daughters sometimes find it equally difficult to escape them.

There is also a different level of reaction, which emanates from our being part of a group, class, race, religion, tribe or nation. If we are honest with ourselves, we all have class, race or group reactions. It is not difficult to apply the predictability test: if you find that your reactions to any economic or political issue are predictable, you can consider yourself in danger of being a prisoner of group thinking of some kind.

In normal times, group reactions can be considered part of ordinary life. When there is polarisation and conflict, they become dangerous. The effect of such reactions can threaten the very fabric of society in a period of transition of power or when, through a shift in generation or the influx of a new population, there is a sudden awareness of existing injustice. The recent flood of refugees from Asia and Africa has brought out amongst some groups in the European population what can best be described as a latent mistrust of foreigners. We also see how in countries like the Lebanon or South Africa many people, who were originally not concerned with being part of one group, have gradually been forced to become conscious of their religion, race or tribal affiliation.

Often it takes an unusual or extraordinary incident to make us discover the depth of our true feelings. I would never have found out how vulnerable and touchy I was, if I had not visited another capital city with other friends and been part of a programme of meetings and conversations where for each event a limited number of participants had to be chosen. By necessity, on some occasions one or other of the visitors had to be excluded. As it happened, there was to be a conversation with a senior political figure in which only four people could participate. That was the moment where it became obvious to me that inclusion or exclusion from the event mattered much more to me than what happened to the illustrious visitor. It took a great deal of honesty – after the event, unfortunately – to sort the issue out.

During the same visit, an evening discussion was devoted to the East-West issue. A diplomatic representative of the host country took a very idealistic view of certain Soviet policies, and I felt compelled to take the opposite stand. (Probably, if the diplomat had taken up a hawkish position, I would have been perfectly capable of taking a quite different stance.) In the beginning, the discussion was quite pleasant, but then it suddenly became heated. And when I looked back next morning, I felt ashamed of myself for having led the conversation in a direction which was wholly unproductive for all concerned. I asked myself why I had done it. I concluded that three things had happened: I had reacted to the somewhat one-sided way the diplomat put his points; then my love of winning an argument had become stronger than the desire to establish a relationship of trust and friendship with the man; finally, I recognised that my political views are often dictated by fear, and that reactions based on fear are good counsellors neither in personal relations nor in international politics.

Can we be free of reactions? No, this seems neither possible nor desirable. The real issue is whether we can know ourselves, our 'blind spots' and our reactions, be open about them and take them as guideposts to deeper truths.

16   The Meaning of Ambition

John Lester

IF WE ARE not clinically depressed, and can act normally, we exhibit a variety of drives which enable us to get things done.

In the world as a whole there are hundreds of millions of people whose sole preoccupation is the struggle to survive. There are too many people who have neither adequate resources nor access to food, clothing and housing. For them life can be unbearably and unjustly hard: yet life is not given up without a great struggle, for the drive to survive is enormously strong and has supported the human race countless times in its collective struggle to develop.

Among those who have enough, who do not face starvation, eviction or bankruptcy, there are a variety of other drives. Some are content simply to care for their families, to ensure that they all have enough to live a fulfilled life. Some strive to be comfortable. Others work in order to be able to enjoy their hobbies; work for them is not an end in itself, nor a means to survival but the means to enjoyment of life. This causes a fairly care-free type of existence. Then there are others who are driven by a sense of responsibility. This often lies at the heart of the motivation of the professions like teaching and medicine.

Freedom allows those who seek a stress-free simple life to find it and enjoy it, and those who are determined to reach the top to attempt it. Ambition is normally the human quality which produces the determination to succeed.

Without people who have had such strong drives, a great deal that has been achieved would never have happened. This is true not only in political life but in sport, business, science and discovery. Without ambition the world would not have advanced so far. Much of what the comfortable enjoy would not be there had it not been for the ambitious men and women who came before them.

Ambition is a natural attribute of man: the way God has

made us. As such, it is a neutral gift, good or bad according to how it is used. It is the drive by which much of value has been achieved; yet it is normally a selfish drive, something which may benefit society but which benefits the ambitious person first and foremost. Therefore it is necessary to ask whether it is the best drive.

In my late teens I met a man who had a great effect on me. He was a black South African leader – a big man in every sense – and we had a meal together. As we tackled the soup, he told me that he had thought the only good white man was the dead one. He then told me of the struggles of his people and how he had decided to hold a major demonstration in Johannesburg. Violence might well have ensued, at a time when it was not commonplace and was largely avoided.

Shortly before it was due to begin, a young Afrikaner student from Stellenbosch had come to his house in the African township – the first white man ever to do so. This young white man said, 'I have come to say sorry, I have blamed you for being violent, but I have remained arrogant. I realise now that it is the arrogance of men like me that has made men like you bitter, and I am sorry.' The black man was astonished. No white man had ever talked to him like this before.

He went to his own people and told them. 'We must delay our demonstration,' he said. 'If what this white man says is true, if white men really can become different, then there may be a better way.' His own people thought he had been bought, so they stabbed him and threw him into the gutter. Fortunately, he reached hospital and his life was saved.

The first person to visit him was this young white man. 'When I saw the anxiety in that young man's eyes, I knew he was genuine, and at that moment the bitterness which had driven me began to evaporate. I began to see that it was not colour that counted but what was going on inside someone's heart. Since then,' he added, 'I have felt that I can care and fight for everyone including people like you.'

I was pole-axed. I had never met anyone like that before. I also dimly realised that if he had been driven by bitterness, he was at least thinking of his people. I was driven by ambition and was only thinking of myself. So I went outside and tried something that I had never done before. I said inwardly, 'God, if you are there, have you got something to tell me?'

For some reason, I began to think of my sister and the games of tennis that we played. I was older than she was and was keen, too. She wanted to learn and saw me as her natural teacher. I wanted only to play with people better than me, who improved my game, and not with people less good who spoilt it. However, I did play with my sister from time to time and she possessed a lot of natural talent – far more than I did for all my keenness. So the time arose when, if my game went off, I could be in danger of losing. So I cheated. I called 'out' when balls were 'in', to preserve my lead. As a result of my experiment in 'listening', I went and told her that I had not played honestly.

It was only years later that I saw the significance of this revelation. The incident I had thought of was a key for me. I had an overwhelming ambition to do well, no matter who got hurt, even if I had to cut corners. The new understanding did not remove ambition. It simply revealed to me that an ambition which had become so strong that it caused me to do things which I knew to be wrong was not acceptable: the end never justifies the means.

It led me to believe that if I was to be sensitive to the spiritual journey as well as to the more obvious paths in life, then that required allowing God to reveal his will for me as far as career was concerned, on which my ambition was focussed.

I studied medicine, really enjoyed it and wanted to do well. Yet perhaps because I was unable to forget this sense of the inner journey, a fresh challenge arose. Day after day I had the persistent thought that I should relinquish my career and offer to work in an unpaid capacity with Moral Re-Armament. Each of us has a unique calling; the point does not lie in what my calling was. But the willingness to take that step was essential on my spiritual journey.

For me this was an agonising thought – and one with which I wrestled for many months. When I finally accepted it, I imagined that medicine had gone for good. That turned out not to be true. But at that moment, possibly because I thought it had, something more profound was given. My sense of loss at seeing the end of my career was transformed by a sense of joy at knowing that I had accepted God's will and been true to the deepest that I knew.

Yet, though I thought at the time that God had broken my ambition by taking away what I had hoped would be a distinguished career, I merely transferred my ambition to doing his work. I worked hard for him, and sought to be successful at his work. I still loved the work more than I loved Christ.

Voluntary workers can be ambitious. They can also be lazy, for there may be no one to assess what they are doing. There is not the same productivity to measure that would be present in industry. The answer to ambition – if it needs an answer – is certainly not laziness.

All this made me think more deeply about the role of ambition. At one level we can say that our free societies owe their freedoms to the opportunities people have been given to prove themselves. Such ambition can, it seems, be used by society for the good of many. But so too can it be used by evil. Hitler and Stalin in this century both harnessed their ambitions to hideous evil.

Freedom has been pioneered by ambitious men, and freedom encourages the flowering of ambition – which is part of the reason why economically and in almost every material way, free societies have grown faster than dictatorships. If, however, ambition can become grossly selfish and if in certain circumstances it can be harnessed to evil, then can it be considered to be the best driving force? Is there indeed an effective alternative?

As I reflected on my career, which I feared I had lost, and on my ambition, which was still present in my work for God, I began to realise that what he was asking me was not simply to work for him but to love him as well. It began to dawn on me that God's own motivation is not ambition but love. Ambition may be fine at one level, but at another it cries out for an answer. That answer is love. Ambition almost inevitably has a 'self' component to it. Love, on the other hand, has no 'self' component, it is all about giving to others.

Ambition remains a means of sustaining and developing the human story. Yet where it becomes overweening, and overrides conscience, it becomes contrary to God's laws. Some of the most powerful and successful thus become shallow personalities. Even for well-intentioned people, busyness can steal the time required for deeper reflection, for God himself. Many in leadership forsake an inner call, or remain in ignorance of it, because they fall for the temptation to succeed at all costs. Such leadership becomes devoid of spiritual content and continues the myth that all the important things in life are material. In our twentieth-century societies, the deeper spiritual dimension has faded. We have refined competition, which is a fruit of ambition, more than care, which is a fruit of love.

Ambitious people will continue to achieve much, but no one, in their own strength, can be the guardians of the deeper values which emerge from faithfulness to conscience and obedience to God.

It is one of the paradoxes of our age that freedom allows us to pursue our ambitions – but that freedom itself is sustained by those deeper spiritual values which we are required to put before our ambition.

With ambition alone our society could become supremely successful and yet decay from within through moral and spiritual weakness, as the Roman Empire did. If we place other values first and therefore place curbs on our ambition, we will nurture freedom, but it could be argued that we may not be so successful materially. This may depend on whether we are the sole architects of our development and whether love really is a more dynamic driving force than ambition. We do, however, face the interesting possibility that if we choose God's values as the means to preserve the freedom on which our prosperity depends, then the quest for material success may no longer seem so important.

17   The Antidote to Bitterness

John Lester

THE SCALE OF suffering in this century, much of it man-made, is almost too great for any individual to encompass. It is not easy to understand what unlocks in the human soul those dark forces which extinguish normal restraint and allow real barbarity to emerge.

Perhaps the most powerful symbol of man's inhumanity to man for our century is to be found in Auschwitz, the very name of which conjures up immeasurable tragedy.

I have a Polish friend who was born more than sixty years ago in a region which is now part of the Ukraine. Aniela was just one more victim of the terrible cruelty that affected ten percent of the Polish population: she was deported to the frozen forests of northern Russia. Fifty years after that deportation, having long settled in Britain, she was finally ready to return to her native land. There, a priest urged her to go to Auschwitz not to stoke up the fires of her bitterness, but to allow her to resolve something that would not be resolved by trying to forget.

'After so many years', she told me, 'it still terrified me. The priest took me to the Wall of Death. We saw the mountain of discarded shoes, the mountain of shaven hair. Suddenly I saw the whole history. I felt that I had to get out. Yet I couldn't move, I was paralysed. I was so frightened of the hatred of the Germans that was in me. They had been for me the worst symbol of evil. I cried out, "My God, my God, help me!" Suddenly I saw the outstretched hands of Christ. I heard his words, "Father, forgive them, for they do not know what they are doing." The words were repeated and then, "I died for them, I died for them." For me it was the greatest victory – not mine but his. Far from being completely beaten, I became a totally new person. At that moment, when I knew I was reborn, the gratitude I felt to God was overwhelming. But what is more important is that I no longer hate. Now I pray for the Germans every day.'[1]

This story reveals poignantly the way of forgiveness, which is one of the possible responses to the suffering caused by the cruelty of others. Another response is that of resignation, which comes from being physically and psychologically overwhelmed; we see it in the faces of those who are left to starve to death in a world in which one half can watch, in comfort, the other half dying.

There is another response, which contrasts with forgiveness: the response of bitterness. While it has been a means used in the struggle for freedom from oppression, it is itself an instrument of oppression. Whilst forgiveness releases the spirit, bitterness imprisons it. It is destructive both of its victims and of the individuals who are possessed by it.

Irina Ratushinskaya, the Russian poet, who was imprisoned by the KGB in the Soviet Union for writing faith-filled poems, said that she and her fellow prisoners were given cause to hate every minute of every day. They were enticed to hate by entirely unwarranted slights and hurts. Until she was in prison, she could not understand why Jesus spoke out so strongly against hatred. In prison she discovered that those who gave in and allowed themselves to hate were eventually destroyed from within. She saw several become mad and others become so damaged that they never recovered.[2]

The relationship of revenge to hatred is very similar to the relationship of orgasm to the sexual appetite. For a while it satisfies the craving of the appetite, but it also feeds it so that it grows, until the bitterness takes over the whole feeling capacity of the human heart.

It often affects physical health as well. I have seen many patients with stomach ulcers caused by bitterness. I am reminded of a woman who was crippled with arthritis: she could neither walk nor write. It emerged that she hated six people who had wronged her. To the suggestion that she might write and ask forgiveness for her bitterness, she replied, 'I can't, because I can't write. My hands are too deformed.' Her friend suggested that she might try.

This she did, writing slowly, painfully and indistinctly. As she wrote, her writing improved and she got quicker. By the time the last letter was written, she had regained the movement in her hands and found herself able to walk again. After that, if ever bitterness overtook her, her arthritis worsened. I do not claim to know the mechanism of this type of experience. It is not all that uncommon; although it would be quite unfair to suggest either that all sufferers from arthritis have some hidden bitterness, or that anyone who is bitter will develop arthritis.[3]

I discovered myself that I had an aversion to women in positions of power, like strong nurses in hospital or parking wardens, but had no idea why. One morning I had taken our baby son to have an inoculation. After the doctor had injected him, a nurse came up and said, 'Now, you will come with me!' Immediately my hackles rose. I felt intense anger and the doctor noticed. 'Why ever are you angry?' he asked. I had no answer, I simply did not know. All I knew was that that one sentence had destroyed my equanimity.

It troubled me that I had no control over my feelings, no defence against a distortion of my judgement, so I prayed and asked if I could be shown what lay behind my reaction. As I prayed, I saw myself as a small child of nearly five. My mother was having a baby at home. A midwife had been sent in to look after her. I had a cold, so the midwife, fearing my mother would catch the infection, had kept me in my room. I wanted to see my mother and my baby sister; she refused to let me go in to my mother's room. Ever since then, whenever someone, particularly a woman, stood between where I was and where I wanted to be, I had lost my temper. An old bitterness was revealed. That was all, but since then the problem has never returned. The insight produced a cure.

A trades unionist I know was sent as a young child to a boys' orphanage. Later he was fostered out to a couple who were keen on the Salvation Army but who were also sadists. They taught him to play the trumpet, but they also tied him to the dining-room chair when he fidgeted and banged him over the head with the family Bible when he misbehaved. For more serious offences they whipped him. The result was a young man who rebelled against religion and turned to Marxism.

Gradually he found his way to a different path. Instead of the Marxist doctrine that the end justifies the means, he turned to Christian moral standards. Instead of aiming to be destructive, he became constructive. He told a group of young people, 'I knew that the people who worked in the orphanage were genuine. Even when I was most rebellious, I could not quite forget their love and their faith – and now it has all been given back again.'

My wife and I lived at one time in a large conference centre. We were responsible for its programme and running. Without realising it, I was dominated by the desire to make a good job of what I was doing. Then someone much older began to take exception to some of my initiatives. Perhaps he was afraid that my ambition could do real damage, perhaps he feared change. Whatever the reason, he began undercutting all I did, and I felt very angry.

I had not learnt how to look at criticism with the humility to accept what was justified and the strength to reject what was not. I seemed only to be able either to reject everything, with great anger, or to accept everything like a doormat, with supressed bitterness. I soon noticed that, although I did not say anything to the person concerned, I found myself arguing with him in my mind. In my bath, I would win every argument. As I walked around, I would brood. I was unable to think of much else.

Fortunately, a wise friend cared enough to talk it all through with me and help me to sort it out with the person concerned. The whole thing melted away and was gone.

Bitterness is always a choice. We cannot avoid being hurt or having injustice heaped on us. Sadly, circumstances make this more likely for some than for others and I count among my friends many who have suffered grievously. But if we choose bitterness we choose something which imprisons us and is harmful, because it finds its consummation in hurting others.

The Northern Ireland scene reveals a cycle of hatred that has never been finally broken through the centuries. As an Englishman I recognise that my country has loaded upon the Irish people much injustice which has provoked and fuelled the hatred. We dominated a Catholic nation and planted it with Protestant settlers largely for strategic reasons. Our policies, determined by our own self-interest, sowed the seeds for the discord which still exists.

We often point a finger of blame at both the Catholic and Protestant Irish communities. Through attacks on our own people, in which innocent victims have died, we have become the third wronged community. Who, therefore, will break the chain of hate?

We English could choose to admit the historic wrongs and apologise for the attitudes which allowed them to happen, in so far as they are still part of our national character. We should be sorry too for those miscarriages of justice which we have allowed to happen in recent times.[4]

Such repentance by those who have caused injustice or perpetrated cruelty breaks the cycle of hatred; as does forgiveness on the part of the victims.

A few years ago an IRA bomb exploded in Enniskillen, Northern Ireland, during a Remembrance Day service. Among the victims was a young nurse who died in the rubble holding her father's hand. Her last words to him were 'I love you.' Her father publicly forgave the bombers for what they had done, knowing that that was what his daughter would also have wanted. It was a story which went far and wide, moved many and did much to build peace between the communities. It prevented revenge killings, demonstrating that forgiveness can break the chain of hate.

There are many individuals and in some cases whole peoples who have suffered hideous wrongs. None of us, especially when we have not had to suffer to the same extent, can demand forgiveness, nor judge those who feel unable to forgive. When forgiveness is freely offered, a great release from the imprisonment of bitterness results.

The journey towards inner freedom is a journey towards love. Hatred has no part in it because hatred and love are opposites. Bitterness and ambition are both powerful drives but in examining bitterness we have arrived at the same conclusion as we did in examining ambition. The alternative to both is the same: it is love.

18   Freedom and 'the Other'

John Lester and Pierre Spoerri

NOT SO LONG AGO, most of us in Western Europe could live our own lives ignoring other classes, races and religions. We knew that they existed, but their troubles or concerns did not need to disturb us nor influence our decisions. We lived safely in the company of our own people. We had our own languages, political instincts, churches, and culture. If there were foreigners around, it was clear that they were outsiders.

The fact that Europe is now multicultural became evident in Britain and France before it penetrated the consciousness of other continental nations. In Germany and Switzerland, it took a long time for people to realise that many of the workers and their families who had been invited to support the booming economies were there to stay and that Berlin, for instance, had become one of the largest Turkish cities in the world.

This, of course, may be just the beginning of an evolution whose end nobody dares to predict. Travelling through Germany and Poland in the beginning of the nineties, the fear of thousands of poor, unemployed refugees and their families streaming over the borders from the East and from the South could be felt everywhere.

The German author Günter Grass in 1989 described in a prophetic scenario what would happen if the cities of the Third World continue to grow as they have done in the last years: 'Around the year 2000, so say the statistics, more than half of mankind will live cheek by jowl in Asia. Migrations of whole people, which have already started and which no power will be able to stop, will change the world and its traditional structures. Concepts based on Europe or on individual nations alone will prove ridiculously inadequate to deal with such an onslaught. However the industrial nations will react, their arrogant pride will have to face the fact: Calcutta stands before the door and will not be turned away.'[1]

The future of freedom in Europe will very much depend on our ability to cope with this kind of challenge. We will have to look at two aspects. Abraham Lincoln said at the time of the American Civil War that no nation can live half-slave and half-free; in our 'global village' we cannot live permanently half-rich and half-poor. Western Europe will be a frontier between rich and poor both to the East – at this point it is going straight through Germany itself – and to the South. The first question is then, whether the prosperous West shows the readiness to share and to sacrifice enough to bridge the growing gap between both these worlds.

The second has to do with history. All of us Europeans will have to look at some pages of our past – as a continent and as a predominantly Christian civilisation – which will be hard to face. The continuing crisis in the Middle East reminds everyone that past injustices seem to reappear on the scene just when everyone hopes that they are permanently forgotten. We have described already how difficult it is to become free of the hurts of history.

When in addition to differences of culture, language and class, religious fundamentalism exercises its polarising power, the potential for conflict can reach dangerous proportions. Diversity can be a great gift, but it is also a potent source of misunderstanding. There are obvious differences between the major religions. What seems more important to us is that there are also definite points of convergence, for example a common agreement on the need for absolute moral standards. From these emerge a concept of goodness and therefore an awareness of the difference between good and evil which is recognised everywhere.[2]

The difference between the religions is heightened because the Christian faith has been widely accepted in the West, which for several centuries has dominated the rest of the world politically, militarily, culturally and commercially. It must be difficult at times for non-Europeans to separate Christ, who for us is universal and who was born in Asia, and his values from other Western cultural values. Not all have the perspective of a Mahatma Gandhi who said that he had a great love for Christ but not so much respect for the Christians. With the rise of materialism it is very hard for other cultures not to feel that religion could even become the back door to a permissiveness which is alien and which they do not want.

So there is a need for great change in us Western Christians, to learn again humility; to shed any desire for domination, any feeling of superiority; to separate our cultural norms from the essentials of our religion; to recognise that while we have something precious to share so too we have plenty to learn; and to recognise God and his handiwork in all religions.

*   *   *

Not everyone has the opportunity to mingle and live with people from different religions, races and backgrounds. But it is only when we meet 'the other' face to face for long enough that we can discover how our nature reacts to this 'otherness'. Until then we can live with the illusion that whilst the world around us is racist and full of prejudice, we are free of all such weaknesses.

John: We had in our home one day a group of health service personnel – doctors, nurses and trades unionists – to discuss the future of the service.

At one point, two people were principally involved in the discussion. A hospital porter said rather cynically to an orthopaedic surgeon, 'You see, we think that you think that you are in some way special.' The consultant was honest enough to say that that was exactly what he did think. He explained that, throughout his training, he had respected his own chief and fitted in with what he had wanted because of his skills and experience. And as he himself worked, he too had climbed the ladder of honour. 'I did not assume', he said, 'that I was worthier than anyone else, but thought that through my hard work, training, skills and diligence, others would look up to me and respect me.'

For years in the National Health Service he had worked harder and longer than required to under his contract. He had done the work willingly as a contribution to society and had never worried how much he was paid for it. All he expected was the loyalty and respect of his staff. 'But suddenly,' he said, 'it has gone. Nobody opens the doors for me now – because who am I to expect it? I am asked to remove my car from my privileged parking spot because I have no right to be privileged. The cup of coffee that was handed out to me has now been withdrawn. It is served in the canteen with everyone else. The operation which was done before whenever I wanted it has to fit in with the wishes of the theatre staff. My status has gone and with it my morale. I had no right to my status, but as it has been taken away, so my desire to do my usual very large load of work has left me.'

The man who chose to reply was a trades union activist. He had had to add an extra job to his regular one for many years to make ends meet. 'I understand,' he began, 'but you're not the only ones to suffer. I turned to the unions 32 years ago because of my sufferings and those of so many people in Britain. You say that work is losing its satisfaction. For millions of us it has never had and cannot have any satisfaction. We do a routine job which is only a means to an end – survival. You say that money doesn't matter. We say how lucky you are. You must earn a great deal of money to feel that it doesn't matter. We have never had enough to be able to say that.

'The hatred you now have of interference has been with us always. People told us first that we must clock in and out, because we weren't trusted. They then locked things out of our way for the same reason, and then they put supervision over us to check on all we did. The bitterness you feel may now help you to understand the bitterness which so many of us have felt for years – the exploitation and the lack of respect and trust for us as individuals.'

Those two men became friends that day and the rest of us gained extra insights about 'the other' and the reality that we were none of us free of prejudice. In almost every country there are people who, for one reason or another, are considered second-class. In Britain, we have to face the fact that through the industrial revolution we produced a stratified society. There are many trades unionists who are frustrated managers: people with the intelligence and strength to manage factories who feel it would be disloyal to leave their own group, who can fight to remove injustices but who still think in terms of their own people and the others, them and us. Those who were in the position of the surgeon should have shown respect and courtesy to those who had not had the same chances in life; that 'stand-offishness' allowed feelings to fester, which found expression, not in raising up everyone to the privilege of the surgeon, but in stripping him down to the level of everyone else; a failure in relationships which, multiplied throughout society, has deeply affected Britain's performance.

Yet one of the precious freedoms we have is the freedom to start again. We do not have to stay the same. This was illustrated for me by the experiences of another trades unionist, Bill, whom I got to know, who was for many years convenor of the sheet metal workers at one of the huge car plants in the industrial Midlands, and a man of great humanity. His family had suffered during the depression years of the thirties. For many years, Bill was driven by his bitterness. His political and trades union work partly flowed from it. In the factory he was regarded as a difficult man by some and as a hero by others.

But something remarkable happened. His brother found a faith in God and became so different that Bill became intrigued and gradually he, too, made a new start. He accepted that it was not 'who was right' that mattered but 'what was right'. He let his bitterness go and began to think of the prosperity of the whole factory rather than just the rights of his members.

One day, in the factory, an unnecessary stoppage became likely. Bill, as one of the convenors, did not know what to do. He had begun to experiment with the idea that if he listened, God might show him what to do. So he took himself off into a corner, putting his hands around his ears to cut out the noise, to seek for inspiration. His friends rushed up, thinking that he was ill. 'No,' he said, 'I'm just listening to God.' They were highly amused and fetched a stretcher, putting him on it and rushing him through the factory, saying, 'Now we know you're ill.' From then on he was called 'The Bishop'.

Some time after this, Bill decided that he needed an office from which he could conduct his work as union convenor. He went to the manager and asked. The manager summoned the supervisor. There was an almighty row. 'You have the nerve to ask for an office, you who have made my life hell. Over my dead body!'

Bill admitted that he had made the supervisor's life hell, but said that he had decided to be different and to start again; he added that he was sorry. The supervisor refused to budge. So Bill said, 'All I can ask is that when you go home you sit in your rocking chair and think if you have ever done anything wrong.' The supervisor came back next day and said that he had sat in his rocking chair and that he too had done things wrong, and that he would be prepared to start again with Bill. Bill got his office.

Some time later, the IRA bombed two pubs in the centre of Birmingham with great loss of life. Feelings ran high in the city. Several of the workers at Bill's factory lost relatives. Several thousand of the workers there were Irish. The next morning a fight broke out on the production track and it was clear that there could easily be a riot and further bloodshed. The Communist convenor of the factory – who had opposed Bill on many issues – rang him and pleaded with him to do something. 'You're the only one who can,' he said. So Bill, after a moment of reflection, rang the management to request a half-hour break. The men stopped the tracks and Bill began a silent march in memory of those who had died. They marched round the whole factory and everyone, including all the management, joined in. Then Bill walked them, like the Pied Piper of Hamelin, out of the factory and on to the huge field where they normally held their mass meetings.

Bill told me afterwards that he did not know what to do next. He stood up and said one sentence to the huge crowd: 'We must not blame a nation for the sins of a few.' Then he started on the Lord's Prayer. 'I'm not used to that sort of thing and I didn't know whether I could remember the words, but everyone joined in.' At the end, there was total silence, and one by one the huge crowd melted away and returned to work. There was no bloodshed.

People from my background were taught that trades

unionists were simply out to make trouble and were not to be trusted. We put them all into the same box, without any first-hand knowledge. Those I came to know as friends helped me to treat them as individuals and respect them for their qualities. In reality, we have far more in common with those we regard as 'the other' than prejudice would have us believe.

* * *

Pierre: I was 26 when I first travelled to Asia. At that time, I thought that coming from Switzerland – a small, neutral country that had never been a colonial power – I would be received by the Asians more warmly than the British or Americans. It took me little time to realise that the fact that I was a member of the white race mattered much more than my citizenship of Switzerland, and that subtle differences like nationality were not of great interest except to a small minority.

During this Indian journey, I had to interpret from English into German and back, night and day, for two German miners who had been long-term members of the Communist Party and had suffered under the Nazis during the war. They had found in Moral Re-Armament something more satisfying than Communism and were keen to pass their experience on to their Indian hosts, especially those from the Indian working class. I had never met a Communist and certainly had no idea how people in the German Ruhr had suffered during the pre-war recession and then the war. Although growing up in a professor's family had, as I thought, given me no sense of class or race superiority, my German companions and their wives clearly felt that something divided us. Was it my language, my education or my often superior way of looking at things? It took time for us to work things out. Finally, a real basis of trust was established, and the friendships with these people have now lasted more than 30 years.

In my relationship to people of other races, cultures and religions I have had to face a multitude of feelings and motivations. It has been relatively easy to recognise active dislike, hatred, fear or mistrust. I found a more subtle paralysing force in cautiousness or indifference.

My personal experience and our national history had not given me any particular view of the Jewish people and of Israel. I did not go out of my way to meet Jews or Israelis if they happened to be in the same place as I was. This situation changed when I married a German and went to live in Germany. Two German friends helped me to face my indifference and to be ready to get involved with people who might well ask me uncomfortable questions and disturb my neutral peace.

One of them had decided at the end of the war that in order to make restitution for what Germany had done to the Jews he would dedicate a good part of his time and energy to building new relations between his country and Israel. He invited me twice to accompany him with a group of Germans to meet a whole cross-section of Israeli society. The other friend who helped me, a Member of the Bundestag, had a close colleague in the U.S. Congress who happened to represent Brooklyn and was an active member of the Jewish community.

My politician friend landed in New York at a moment of acute crisis between the German government and the American Jewish leaders. The Congressman from Brooklyn asked the German politician to speak in his synagogue after the religious service on the Sabbath. When the German stood up in front of these men, he realised that their eyes were asking, 'Where was this man in 1933, when Hitler took power? Where was he during the war? Was he an active Nazi? What did he do to the Jews?' He plunged straight in: 'Before the war I was an enthusiastic member of the Hitler Youth.' An old man in the back shouted, 'And he even admits it!' The German asked, 'Would you like me to be like all those who say that they never had any part in anything that happened?'

He then went on with his story, describing how as an officer cadet in what is now Poland, he and his comrades had to exercise on a field near a railway-yard. One day, two trains pulled up, and a group of haggard and miserable people were driven by SS officers from one train to the other. The young cadets were upset and asked their commander what was going on. His reply was short: 'Don't worry, they're only

Poles and Jews!' The German added, 'I still feel deeply ashamed that I just accepted that statement.'

As a result of this and many other painful encounters, the German politician became a personal friend of several Jewish leaders who had themselves been prisoners in Auschwitz. Through many meetings on both sides of the Atlantic, these men helped to bring some fresh perspective to the strained triangular relations between Germany, the United States and Israel.

While accompanying friends like this German politician on their personal and political journey, I could not remain indifferent or neutral myself. Even if much of what these Germans and Jews had lived through was beyond my experience, I did not feel divided from them. I had much to learn from them, and I was also able to work with them towards a common goal.

* * *

For many of us, the issue of 'the other' will not involve conflicts in distant lands but people much closer to home. In Germany, refugees, asylum seekers and immigrants from German-speaking regions of Eastern Europe are in evidence in practically every town and village. A friend of ours discovered that a family of German origin coming from Russia was unable to find any accommodation and was forced to live for an indefinite time in a camp. Our friend decided to receive this family in his own home and shared with them home and kitchen for several months until permanent lodgings could be found.

The future of freedom in Europe and beyond will very much depend on the way we learn to live with 'the other'. Direct contact and dialogue are steps which may be open to most of us. Another step may have to do with power, in the life of the individual and the life of nations.

19 Freedom and Power

Pierre Spoerri

IN CONSIDERING THE role of sex, ambition and bitterness in our personal lives, and the influence of class, culture and religion in our collective lives, we touch on the issue of power: the power of individuals and of groups and nations.

The twentieth century has been marked by some of the most ruthless and systematic forms of power in history. Of these the power of ideological dictatorship that conditions the lives of whole nations down to the smallest detail of individual existence, often permanently distorting habits and attitudes and using fear as its greatest weapon, has been the most horrific. More subtle is the power of multinational companies and organisations in shaping national and international economic policies. But power is also a factor, a conscious or unconscious one, in each individual life.

One difficulty, of course, is that the word power has so many meanings. Brian Crozier writes in *The Masters of Power*, 'For the English language, normally so rich, is defective in this area: as M. Raymond Aron and others have noted, "power" means both *puissance* (as in "great power") and *pouvoir* (as in "to be in power"). To add to the confusion, "power" also means *énergie* (as in hydro-electric power). My definition of "power" ', Crozier adds, 'is what individuals and governments *can get away with*.'[1]

Crozier's definition confirms the feeling of many good responsible citizens that power as such is something almost sinister. Many Christians do not like the word power, saying in prayer the words 'the power and the glory are yours' but preferring not to have too concrete an idea of what this is all about. Most of us will agree with Abraham Lincoln's saying that 'nearly all men can stand adversity, but if you want to test a man's character, give him power.' But our instinct responds even more to Lord Acton's statement that 'power tends to corrupt; and absolute power corrupts absolutely.'

Power, for those without it, has most of the time an authoritarian, rather destructive feel to it. If you handle power, their instincts tell them, you are bound to get your hands dirty.

The result is that many good, religious people honestly think that faith and politics cannot go together, that as a person of faith the less one has to do with public life the better. The reputation of politicians often encourages those who keep out of the public eye to be violent critics of those who remain in it. It even seems to offer a kind of satisfaction to some people to 'keep their hands clean' and then to blame others for making mistakes. With 'media politics' gaining more and more ground, there is even more reason for good men and women not to enter public life: why open yourself to abuse when a public career already demands so many sacrifices of time and energy and private life?

But a vacuum of political leadership and the risk of anarchy can be as dangerous for a country as dictatorship; this has been shown again in the late eighties and early nineties when Eastern European and African governments, many run by corrupt Communist parties or equally corrupt military regimes, crumbled, but there were not enough trained people ready to take their place.

Father Jozef Tischner, one of the spiritual leaders of the Polish Solidarity movement wrote, 'When I do not know who rules me, I do not know who I am. And it is my duty to know who I am.'[2]

Even for those who are not directly concerned with politics, there are some facts concerning power that sooner or later have to be faced.

* The exercise of power is an integral part of human nature; consciously or unconsciously we all exercise power over others and have to submit to the power of others. There is the power of sexual attraction, which is often exploited in many ways, and not just by one side. There is sheer muscular power. And there is a more subtle approach to power. People speak of 'threatening' and 'non-threatening' personalities: using stature, strength of voice or sharpness of argument to exercise power over others.

One of the deep thinkers of the post-World War II era, Romano Guardini, wrote in *Die Macht* (Power): 'Every act, every situation, even the very fact of life, of being is directly or indirectly linked to the consciousness of exercising or enjoying power. In its positive form, this means to become conscious of our self-reliance and our strength. In its negative form, it leads to arrogance, pride and vanity.'[3]

* For all of us it is essential to know the basics of the mechanism of division of power or power-sharing. This issue is relevant in family life as well as in the plans to reform European institutions. How much power needs to be invested in 'central government' (be it the paterfamilias or the Brussels Commission) and how much has to be shared with the member units?

* There exists a liberating power that can fundamentally transform human nature and human relationships. It is a power that is too often ignored in the name of realism and *Realpolitik*.

Life in a political capital like Bonn offers many illustrations of the truth that power is a fickle mistress. A Member of the Bundestag who has worked here since the sixties once said to me, 'In this city, if you really want to get to the top, you have to be ready to sacrifice everything, including your family. I wasn't ready to do that, so I chose consciously to stay in the second rank.' Another said, 'If my party tries to force me to do something that goes against my conscience, I can always return to my farm. But I don't envy those who have no job and no security to fall back on.'

For many people engaged in political life there comes the moment when they have to decide how far they will let other people or the system control them, and when the moment has come to say 'enough is enough'. One American friend, a Congressman, knew that a stand on an issue of civil rights could well cost him his seat. Many people encouraged him to compromise. He took his stand and lost; but he never regretted his decision, as he remained an inwardly free personality. The same happened to a friend who sat on the opposition benches of the Polish Sejm for nineteen years. The moment came when the Communist government wanted to push through a constitutional amendment which he considered totally wrong; he was the only member who voted against it, and as a result he was pushed out of political life. Twenty years later, in June 1989, when the Communists lost their monopoly of power, he was triumphantly re-elected as a Senator. He would never have been given that chance if he had compromised with power two decades earlier.

The first to praise the virtues of a division of power in the organisation of a state – between the executive, the legislative and the judiciary – was the French writer and philosopher Montesquieu. The political upheavals of the late eighties and early nineties have shown again the importance of this principle. Andrei Sakharov said during one of the last meetings of the Supreme Soviet which he attended that that body had not solved its 'key political task' as it had not dared to face the need for a clear division of power in the new constitution. 'As long as this political task is not fulfilled,' he added, 'it remains practically impossible to develop real solutions for the complex of urgent economic, social, national and ecological problems.'[4] No doubt many of his countrymen will recognise that this statement remains valid whatever constitutional form the successor nations to the Soviet Union adopt.

German reunification created the need to adapt the constitutional basis of German democracy, and directed the attention of politicians, editorial writers and ordinary people again to the links between human nature, the division of power and the functioning of democratic institutions. There was astonishingly general agreement that the post-war 'Basic Law', the constitution of the German Federal Republic, had worked well. One of the shrewdest observers of the post-World War II years wrote, 'It was not confidence but scepticism that characterised the work on that constitution. The measure was not the infallibility of the people, which tyrants often refer to, but the fallibility of human nature.

'The attitude of the members of the Constitutional Council resembled in this very much the one that controlled the fathers of the American Constitution.'[5] James Madison, one of the writers of that Constitution, commented, 'But what is government itself, but the greatest of all reflections on human nature? If men were angels, no government would be necessary. If angels were to govern men, neither external nor internal controls on government would be necessary. In framing a government which is to be administered by men over men, the great difficulty lies in this: you must first enable the government to control the governed; and in the next place oblige it to control itself.'[6] But division of power does not just operate in politics. We have all experienced some form of power-sharing in the family. Most of us know the situation where one member of the family exercises power unjustly or where either the parents or the children try to achieve full control over the others. In the family and in organisations, as in politics, whenever too much power – executive power, financial power, intellectual power – is concentrated in too few hands, abuses are inevitable. Checks and balances seem to be an essential need if the less pleasant sides of human nature are to be kept under control and freedom is to be preserved.

There does exist a great liberating power that can transform us, and perhaps the situations around us, from inside. I saw this power at work in a politician whom I got to know well during the last years of his political career in Bonn. During this time, he discovered the conflict of power and faith. So he took time every morning to examine in the light of his Christian faith what had happened the previous day and what was ahead of him. As time went on, he became aware of three pitfalls. One was simple vanity. Some responsible person in party or government had only to say, 'You are the only person capable of doing this,' and already he had taken on a job which, in the depth of his heart, he did not feel was really his.

The second pitfall was his family. For a long time, politics always won over the concerns of home. But when he saw how many of his colleagues' families suffered from this kind of neglect, he decided that the needs of his family would have priority over everything else. His third pitfall was snobbery. One day he decided to have a conversation with an ordinary person outside the political 'circus' every day. This helped him to realise what people were really thinking; it also kept him humble. During his last years in the German Bundestag, he was regarded by colleagues of all parties and by people outside as 'the voice of conscience of the parliament'.

Those of us who are Christians will call this liberating force God or the redeeming power of Jesus Christ. Others will find another name for it. Guardini writes, 'Jesus deals with human power as the reality it is. He also understands it; otherwise the third temptation, which is a temptation of hubris (Matthew 4, 8-10), would have no meaning ... But he sets humility, arising from an inner source, as liberating force against the domination of power ... Redemption does not mean that circumstances in the world change once and for all, but that in God is the constant source of new life.[7]

This transforming power is clearly not under our control. But it is available when we give it a chance to operate in us and around us. It is the only power that can heal hurts and overcome hate and bitterness. It is the power we need to understand and experience if we want to advance as individuals and as a human race.

20   The Paradox of Love

John Lester

THE TRAGEDY OF our age is that, whilst we know more than any generation before us about the physical world we live in, we know less about the world of the Spirit which was deeply researched and understood by some of our forebears.

There are plenty of us who love music. A few are gifted performers: and fewer still, who have a profound sense of music, stand out as composers or interpreters, musicians' musicians. There are many others who cannot tell one note from another; they hear, yet they do not hear.

I enjoy paintings and can appreciate them; but I cannot paint, though I wish I could. On the other hand, I have always found mathematics easy – at least to a certain level. As I became involved in higher mathematics, I began to realise that I had limitations: I do not have the gifts that real mathematicians have. But whatever those of us who are neither musical, artistic nor mathematical may say, there is both truth and beauty in music, art and mathematics. The same is true of faith. Sadly, many think they are 'tone-deaf' to this too. It need not be so. It is difficult to understand the profounder paradoxes surrounding human liberty without struggling to attain some spiritual insight.

Since humans first inhabited the earth we have used our minds to ask, 'Why are we here?' The search to make sense of our presence, to invest it with meaning, and to understand something of the Creator of the universe has been pursued in many different ways. Both the search for meaning and the instinct to worship have always been powerful drives.

In Jewish tradition, through the history of one group of people, the Tribes of Israel, the idea grew of one God, a father-figure, awesome, all-powerful, judging but just, to whom every person could relate. This was a monumental leap from the previous concept of many competing gods. The Jews had moved beyond questioning whether a Creator existed to clarifying their relationship with him. From this root came not only modern Judaism but also Christianity and Islam.

A number of elements, which have arisen through Christian thought and understanding, help to clarify the nature of the inherent paradoxes of freedom.

St John wrote in his Gospel 'For this is how God loved the world: he gave his only Son.'[1] This revelation, that the nature of God is love, and that the coming of Jesus was a manifestation of that love, represented a new understanding, which built upon the original Jewish teaching.

It meant that religious life was not simply a question of principles and morals, important though they may be, but involved reaching for a relationship with God. The whole of Jesus' life develops this theme, and through his death and resurrection, Christians believe, mankind is reconciled with God. God's love has included *his* forgiveness of *us*.

This also reveals that God has a will, that there is purpose in all he does. When Jesus was in the Garden of Gethsemane[2] he knew that if he did not turn back, he would certainly be killed. None the less he prayed, 'not my will but yours be done'. People down the ages have recognised that God's will may, as it did with Jesus, run counter to their own; this is part of the experience of the Cross.

In the secular world there are three techniques for getting people to change their views. The first is argument, the second pressure, the third violence. And yet there are countless experiences recorded of men and women who have been changed from within; whose lives have been transformed as a result neither of argument nor of pressure; who have chosen freely to follow God's will. Sometimes that change has occured suddenly and sometimes over the course of a life-time.

St Paul persecuted the early Christians, and watched the first Christian martyr, Stephen, being stoned to death. But on the road to Damascus he suddenly 'met Christ'. This experience, recounted in the *Acts of the Apostles*,[3] includes the three elements of a recognition of the love of God, a feeling of being healed in his relationship with him, and an acceptance of his will. It had nothing to do with rational argument nor with pressure. Paul spent the rest of his life in Christ's service, building up the early churches.

John Wesley had a similar experience in 1738, describing his heart as 'strangely warmed'.[4] Frank Buchman, who in 1908 also experienced something of the same kind, wrote, 'It produced in me a vibrant feeling, as though a strong current of life had suddenly been poured into me and afterwards a dazed sense of a great spiritual shaking up.'[5]

As I have read about the saints like Francis of Assisi,[6] Clare[7] and Thérèse of Lisieux,[8] what has been revealed is not a duty nor a task but a love affair with Christ: men and women who so submit to God's presence that they become lost in him, and begin to reflect Christ himself.

I have often felt conflicting emotions about such experiences: both a drawing towards and a recoiling from them. There is something immensely attractive about the lives of those who have dared to give everything, and yet the prospect is frightening, for it seems to spell the end of 'self'. It is one thing to give to God free time, even ambition and career or questions of money and marriage, but to give your self is surely to lose your identity, perhaps the greatest fear a person can have.

Surely, this kind of giving is the ultimate in imprisonment, the very opposite of freedom? The mystery is that it is not so. The experiences of so many testify to the fact that in daring to let go of self completely it is possible to find true identity and freedom.

St Paul, after his experience on the road to Damascus, described himself as a 'prisoner' of Jesus Christ,[9] and that seems very reasonable. He chose to go God's way, he incurred all sorts of hardships, including shipwreck and physical imprisonment in Rome. His behaviour changed. He accepted entirely new disciplines and limitations to his own choices, but he did it neither from duty, nor from coercion; he wanted to, because he had experienced God's love. His writings reveal him as a free man, happy in what he was doing, who would have chosen no other course. The paradoxical message of Christian teaching is revealed – that such 'slavery' is the route to inner liberty. Freedom is seen not only to have a moral component, as we have seen in earlier chapters, but a spiritual component also.

The real meaning of freedom is revealed in one word –

love. Love is something we can admire and aspire to, yet it is often not quite reachable. In its fullest sense it is not a natural attribute of humans. Rather it is the nature of God, only available to us as a gift, as part of our relationship with him and as we reflect his love on to others. It is as if, in being taken into a relationship with God, we experience something of his nature.

We have built into us a certain portion of love – enough perhaps to whet our desire for it and help our understanding of it. There is the love of parent for child, and the love between two people which is consummated in marriage. These can help us to understand more of God. Even the best things can sometimes become tainted, but it is within the family that most people understand what they know of love. The bonding within a family gives some clue to the nature of God's love for every person.

These experiences of love, while they are not universal, are not out of the ordinary. It is when love expands to embrace more of the human family that it begins to reflect God's love for us all.

I have two friends whose father was an army padre in the Second World War. He was with his men in a troopship. Quite a number were on hammocks in the hold of the ship. The ship developed engine trouble and became separated from the rest of the convoy; it was spotted by an enemy submarine and struck by a torpedo.

As the ship listed and began to fill with water, everyone was urged to take to the boats, and many escaped. But the padre thought of his soldiers, whose 'shepherd' he was, some of whom were wounded when the torpedo exploded, and who had no way of getting out. He asked to be lowered to them on a rope. At first, no one would let him go down, for he was sealing his own fate. Finally they agreed. He went down on the rope and stayed with the men, talking, praying and singing hymns with them. That was the last anyone saw of him.

That is love. That young padre reflected faithfully the love of God for those men.

Most people are never presented with that kind of ultimate challenge. Yet countless such actions over the centuries have ensured that 'divine' love is known in the world, even if most of us do not recognise it very often.

Perhaps this is the basic struggle in the world. Will our negative human qualities – ambition, lust, bitterness, greed – dominate and become the engine of society, or will love be allowed to become the driving force?

Other motives produce partial change. Bitterness produces change, but it favours some and destroys others. The pursuit of greed has made the material wealth of the world greater, but while some have gained others have not. Ambition has brought some to the top but on the shoulders of those who have not made it.

Love is the only force which is universal, which leaves no one out, which treats all the same, which seeks nothing in return. It is the purest motive of all. But it is only available to us as we turn to God, in a humble and profound way. Love produces peace within people, that is its nature. It also confronts evil. Its power, which is the power of the Holy Spirit,[10] is revealed through the lives of those who embrace it.

John Wesley, for example, in the 50 years which followed his conversion regularly preached at 5 am, having risen at 4 am, to crowds of 20-30,000. He travelled 250,000 miles, mostly on horseback, preached 40,000 sermons, wrote grammars of English, French, Latin, Greek and Hebrew, an English dictionary, histories of Rome, England and the Church from earliest times, and had a profound and lasting effect on the social and religious life of Britain.[11]

Love produces freedom, above all freedom from self, which allows people to become single-minded and wholly given. To take an example from our own time: we know that Mother Teresa, in her care for the poor, is free. She is not worried by what others think of her or by the fact that she has no money. She is free to do whatever she wants. Because she loves God, she does not want to do anything other than to care for the poor. She serves others neither from duty nor for any reason other than love.

Love transforms motives so that what we want is not what we wanted before. It is not just a philosophy or a set of principles, it is a relationship with God which transforms us so that we begin to want freely what is pleasing to him.

Inner freedom is at the very core of God's love and its 'imprisonment'. The cost of experiencing that freedom is the abandonment of self in favour of God, submission to the imprisonment of God's will. The resulting experience of joy and love is one of liberation. A heart which loves is a heart which is free.

21   Free to Care

John Lester and Pierre Spoerri

WE HAVE SET DOWN in this book some of the spiritual elements of freedom, because we are aware of the extent to which they have been marginalised and misunderstood. Secular and sacred views clash over the reality of objective moral standards. We believe that the fundamental issue of the age remains whether we will or will not accept the sovereignty of God.

We have concentrated on inner freedom and stressed what it takes to be freed from all that binds us. To be 'free from' is neither an end in itself, nor just a means to our peace of mind. It is the essential means of enabling us to be 'free for' or 'free to'. The person who is 'free from' himself or herself can look afresh at the world to see what to do for it.

At times what we have written may have sounded contradictory. John writes on freedom from ambition, which can sound like a recipe for withdrawing from our competitive and complex society. Pierre writes about the reality of power and the requirement of those of goodwill to stay in the fray. In reality these two views do not conflict, because what we argue for is neither withdrawal nor participation but a change in motivation.

Above all, we argue that freedom from the restrictions on our inner liberty leaves us free, if we will, to obey the inner call of God. For some that may mean an apparent withdrawal; a friend has recently, after much thought, entered an enclosed Carmelite convent. Other friends are deeply involved in politics and remain close to the centre of power. Where the choices in a life arise out of a response to an inner call, then that life will never be one of retreat; it will always be part of God's purposes for the world.

Looking at the world today, it is easy enough to think only in material and sociological terms: all will be well if the world can effect the changes which are obviously required.

144

This is rather different from the thinking of Cardinal Newman who wrote, 'God has created me to do him some definite service; he has committed some work to me which he has not committed to another. I have my mission – I may never know it in this life, but I shall be told it in the next.'[1] Here is a philosophy which holds that God himself has intentions for this world which are not necessarily revealed; they will embrace the material as well as the spiritual, but are clearly more than the sum of our efforts to influence for the better the world in which we live. Such purpose is both real and beyond us. We can be drawn into it, but it is not dependent on our own imagination or reason. It will include the work of the nun who prays and the politician who holds power. The meaning of inner freedom is thus discovered in what it frees us both to be and to do.

Can we do something about the world we live in? In totalitarian societies one of the difficulties was the feeling that nothing could be done about the situation. And yet something was done. In many of the new democracies that burden of impotence has been lifted. Watching from the West, we linked the change from Communist to democratic societies with the definite actions of known individuals. Lech Walesa, Anna Walentinowicz and the Pope all played a decisive part in the liberation of Poland. Václav Havel, Father Václav Maly and the students of the Academy of Arts in Prague played a similar role in Czechoslovakia. In each of these countries the movement towards democracy started with individual decisions. As in the West, there can still be a feeling of impotence even after the establishment of democratic structures. But the individual remains the key. Each person can do something, can make a difference.

During this century we have lived through a chapter of history in which one climax has followed another. At the beginning of the century each one of the major powers was convinced that it had a 'civilising mission' to fulfil. In Britain there were many who assumed that the Empire would continue until the world was changed for the better: a view understandably not held by everyone else, but nonetheless genuine. A few years later, John Mott, the evangelist, talked of 'winning the world for Christ in one generation'.[2] At the beginning of the First World War many assumed that it was the war to end all wars. Communists believed that Communism would transform the world and cause 'the state to wither'. More recently, after the Second World War which seemed to usher in a new world order, millions feared an atomic holocaust that would end the world for ever.

This sense of both the climactic and the apocalyptic led people to believe not only that the world could be changed 'in one generation' but also that it must. The climactic sense of history is passing, partly because what we have hoped for or feared has moved away as we approached it and remains unreachable.

People have become confused about what can be achieved, and whether there are any longer 'grand designs' to which we can give our whole heart, mind and energy. We have witnessed in the past great tides of history, moments when for good or evil the masses have been caught up in something which either elated them or which they felt powerless to stop. Great aims may not always be attainable, but they produce greatness; small aims produce mediocrity. Along with the decline of the climactic has gone the decline of the heroic.

Whilst we live in an age which is enabled to know more than any other, which has unbelievable possibilities before it, it remains an age which finds large goals difficult. It distrusts the heroic approach, and favours individualism rather than mass movements. For such an age the question becomes: is there a grand design which is comprehensible and acceptable to this generation? Is there something, however unclear, which can catch the imagination? Does our freedom allow us the freedom to dream?

There are great material issues in the world which are the responsibility of us all. One of the most important is bridging the gap between the rich and poor countries. This immediately breaks down into a whole host of different but interconnecting issues; and poverty needs to be addressed not only between nations but within nations. Another issue centres on the environment. What are we doing to planet earth? Will we recklessly use all of our non-renewable resources and spoil air and water with pollutants? Can we justifiably hand on to another generation an earth less well endowed than we received?

Then, there are the social issues, such as health, unemployment, homelessness and urban renewal. All these and many more need to tax our imaginations. Some will feel charged to deal with one or more of them. No one can take on all; but the combined efforts of men and women of goodwill must surely triumph in some areas. These are some of the things which we are 'free to' tackle.

And yet somehow it all falls short of the longing in many people for some great vision to bind us together, something which simplifies issues rather than only revealing them in their great complexity; something which is beyond our reach. One of the difficulties may be that we have become so attuned to the material that we are not used to seeing with the eye of spiritual sight.

If we try to look with that eye of faith, what is revealed?

We acknowledge first of all God's love for us, from which flows a growing love for him. Springing from this grows a love for all his people, a love for our neighbour in the widest sense: a calling to care for people in some area of the world or some area of life; a multiplicity of callings which spring from the same motivation. We also develop a love of God's creation.

From this new motivation springs also the desire to obey, not people but the will of God, as revealed through the creative promptings of the inner voice. A visionary of the last century, Henry Drummond,[3] suggested that such obedience is the organ of spiritual knowledge. It is obedience to God which reveals to some degree the grand design, through the recognition that God has a purpose for our world and all it contains, and for all of us. That purpose may not be discernible in its fullness, yet it is the bond which can hold us together; we can become part of that purpose, which is real even though not wholly understood. It offers a unity which springs from our being in relationship with God. This does not depend on our belonging to the same organisations, holding the same views or taking on the same tasks. It is something which is beyond us.

Love is beyond us; moral standards are beyond us; God's purpose is beyond us; our unity is to be found in our common relationship with that which is beyond us. This is so different from those who take the view that there is nothing beyond us. The spiritual stance takes in all the material perspectives and adds something more.

The attempt to form a grand design in material terms fails today in an age which has rejected the utopian perspective, because there are so many different topics to occupy our attention. The purpose which faith furnishes is unknowable and yet does satisfy the craving for meaning and for integration with other people.

It is, of course, impossible to believe that God's purposes do not include answering the material needs of mankind. Yet we have to get used to understanding that that may not be the only point, nor even the main point.

How we relate to this world and its need may be our preparation for the world to come, which is part of what is real but beyond us. God has given us free choice, and we live with the consequences of those choices. Poverty, for example, does not arise by itself. As one of the founders of the British labour movement, Keir Hardie, wrote, 'Poverty is the product of wrong relationships between people.' What we do about both poverty and the faulty relationships may not only benefit the poor; it may also be the means of growth in our own characters.

The world we know is handed on to us as it is because of the choices of others before us. We cannot affect the choices which have been made nor their consequences. But we have now the chance to bring the world more into accordance with God's intentions, as far as we can perceive them. That is our task while on earth, and our preparation for what is to come. We have to leave it to others to take the human story further still; and they can grow in character and grace regardless of how the world is today. God may never have intended a perfect world; if he had, he would not have given us free will, which inevitably causes it to be spoiled at the same time as it is improved. In one sense every generation gains from previous generations, and in another always starts again. In each age this world is the anvil on which God forges souls; or, in Christian terminology, brings them to a state of grace.

God is presumably concerned about poverty and injustice,

though he has allowed them as a consequence of offering us free will. But he is also concerned with repentance, forgiveness and love, the spiritual means which lead to the eradication of both poverty and injustice. If God is interested in souls then so should we be too. To help someone to find God may be the most important and rewarding work in which we can be included, and may also be the means by which many material problems will be solved.

Simple care for people, sharing our own spiritual needs to help others to become open to God – whether it is called evangelism, care, soul surgery, life-changing or some quite new name – touches the material as much as the spiritual.

The ends do not justify the means. But it is worth looking at the obverse: that the means may be the end. God's ways may be seen in his means. The materialist often seeks short cuts to a perceived end. The person who seeks God may recognise that in the means towards achieving a goal God may have hidden his ends.

This is not an easy truth to accept; yet God may be working his purpose out as we undertake the things he calls us to do, not only by achieving the aims but in the means we use to achieve them, in our genuine care for people, in our longing for them to find God.

Freedom to care is the greatest freedom of all. It is greater than the chance to be ourselves, to be free from interference, to be able to express ourselves. It implies different things for different people. It can mean being free to serve, to give to others, to make a better world for our children to live in; to restore relationships, to tackle the legacies of bitterness in the world, the poverty, the disease; to discover, to invent, to create.

At its deepest level it leaves us free to be obedient to the whispers of God, to be open for the world beyond, to be sensitive to his purposes. It frees us to know him. That, in a world which thinks it knows so much, is the fundamental need: the challenge, the hope, of our age.

References and Notes

Quotations from the Bible are taken from the *New Jerusalem Bible*

Chapter 1, Freedom in Captivity and Dictatorship

1. Václav Havel, *Letters to Olga* (Faber & Faber, London, 1988)
2. *The Observer*, 25.3.90.
3. Vladimir Bukovsky quoted in Leif Hovelsen, *The Relevance of Human Rights* (unpublished manuscript).
4. Czeslaw Milosz, *The Captive Mind* quoted in J A C Brown, *Techniques of Persuasion* (Pelican Books 1963).
5. Pavel Kohout quoted in Jürgen Serke, *Das neue Exil* (Fischer Taschenbuch, Frankfurt 1985) p 110.
6. Quoted in Mary Craig, *The Crystal Spirit* (Hodder & Stoughton, London 1986).
7. *The Times*, 6.2.90.
8. Viktor Frankl, *Trotzdem Ja zum Leben sagen* (DTV Munich 1982) pp 107-109.
9. Vladimir Zelinsky, in a speech given in Caux, Switzerland, July 1989.
10. Mihailo Mihailov, *Underground Notes*; in *Mystical Experiences of the Labour Camps* (Routledge and Kegan Paul, London 1977).

Chapter 2, Free to Listen

1. Frank N D Buchman (1878-1961), initiator of the world work of Moral Re-Armament.
2. The earliest known source for this quote is Zeno of Citium, 300 BC: 'The reason why we have two ears and only one mouth is that we may listen the more and talk the less.'
3. Frank Buchman was indebted to the evangelist Henry Wright for this summary of Christ's moral teaching. These standards had originally been set out in *The Principles of Jesus* by Robert Speer (1902). Henry Wright described them as 'the fourfold touchstone of Jesus and the apostles'. He listed his sources as: Purity – Matthew 5, 27-32; Honesty – John 8, 44-46; Unselfishness – Luke 14, 33; Love – John 15, 12 (*The*

151

Will of God and a Man's Lifework 1909). Taken from Garth Lean, *Frank Buchman: a Life* (Constable 1985) chapter 8, p 76 and footnote.

4. Morton T Kelsey, *The other side of Silence* (Paulist Press, New York, 1976) pp 22-23, 100-101.

5. Klaus Bockmühl, *Listening to the God who Speaks* (Helmers & Howard, Colorado Springs 1990) p 151.

Chapter 3, What are we Afraid of?

1. William Wilberforce, 1759-1833, British Member of Parliament, who worked successfully for the abolition of the slave trade and slavery. See also Garth Lean, *God's Politician, William Wilberforce's Struggle* (Darton, Longman and Todd 1980).

2. See Mary Craig, *The Crystal Spirit* (Hodder and Stoughton 1986), chapter 25.

Chapter 4, Healing the Past – Preparing the Future

1. Moral Re-Armament: The programme of Moral Re-Armament was launched by Dr Frank Buchman in East London in 1938, at a time when the European nations were rearming militarily. He called for a world-wide mobilisation of the moral and spiritual forces which urgently needed to be given a rallying point and a philosophy. See *Remaking the World* (Blandford Press 1961) p 45. Moral Re-Armament is currently active on all five continents. For further reading see Garth Lean, *Frank Buchman: a Life* (Constable London 1985).

2. Alfred Grosser, *Le Crime et la mémoire* (Flammarion, Paris 1989) p 155.

3. Richard von Weizsäcker, *Die deutsche Geschichte geht weiter* (DTV, Munich 1985) p 167.

4. Alfred Grosser, op. cit., pp 122-3.

5. *Frankfurter Allgemeine Zeitung*, 11.10.89.

6. *International Herald Tribune*, 11.10.86.

7. Garth Lean, *Frank Buchman: a Life*. (Constable, London 1985), pp 341-384.

8. Winston Churchill, quoted in Paul Johnson, *A History of the Modern World* (Weidenfeld Paperbacks, London 1984), p 599.

9. Weidenfeld/Zimmermann, *Deutschland-Handbuch* (Bundeszentrale für politische Bildung, Bonn 1989) p 99; Erich Schwinge, *Bilanz der Kriegsgeneration* (N.G. Elwert Verlag, Marburg, 1979) p 77.

10. *International Herald Tribune* 16.1.90; also *Bulletin of the Press and Information Office of the German Government*, 17 March, 1990.

11. *Worte der Versöhnung* (Words of Reconciliation), Declaration of the Bishops of Germany and Czechoslovakia, 5.9.90.

12. *German-Polish Dialogue.* (Edition Atlantic Forum, Bonn, Brussels, New York 1966) p 18.
13. *Frankfurter Allgemeine Zeitung,* 6.10.86.
14. *Frankfurter Allgemeine Zeitung,* 28.11.89.

Chapter 5, The Way to Forgiveness and Reconciliation

1. Basil Entwistle, *Japan's Decisive Decade* (Grosvenor Books, London 1985) p 149.
2. *The Japan Times* 25.5.90.
3. Entwistle, op. cit., p 175.
4. Joseph V. Montville, *Track Two Diplomacy, The development of non-governmental peace-promoting relationships,* (Washington 1985) pp 17-18.
5. R C Mowat *Creating the European Community* (Blandford Press, London 1973) p 60.
6. *Time,* 10.10.83.
7. *Frankfurter Allgemeine Zeitung,* 30.4.85.

Chapter 6, Are we Free to Choose?

1. Dieter E Zimmer, *Das sogenannte Unbewusste* (*Zeitmagazin,* 1.11.85) p 42.
2. Paul Johnson, *A History of the Modern World* (Weidenfeld Paperbacks, London 1984) p 11.
3. Paul Johnson, op. cit., p 4 and p 10.
4. Dieter E Zimmer, op. cit., p 46.
5. R Dawkins, *The Selfish Gene* (Oxford University Press 1976).
6. Hubert Markl, *Im Labyrinth der Gene - Zwischen Erbanlagen und Freiheit* (*Frankfurter Allgemeine Zeitung* 12.10.85).
7. See *Spektrum der Wissenschaft* December 1985.
8. Charles Rubia, interview with Herbert Cerutti in *NZZ-Folio* (Zurich March 1992) p 35.
9. Thomas Mann, quoted in Viktor Weisskopf, *The Joy of Insight* (Basic Books – Harper/Collins 1991) p 318.
10. C F von Weizsäcker, *Das Prinzip höherer Einfachheit, Albert Einstein z 100sten Geburtstag* (*Die Zeit* 10.3.79).
11. Armin F Barth, *Denkende Maschinen und ihre künstliche Intelligenz* (*Neue Zürcher Zeitung,* 5.9.90).
12. Peter Haffner and Otmar Schmid, *Gehirngespinste - Portrait: Valentin Braitenberg* (*Zeitmagazin,* 22.6.90).
13. Paul Tournier, *The Meaning of Persons,* translated by Edwin Hudson, (SCM Press, 1957) p 218.

154 Rediscovering Freedom

Chapter 8, Materialism: the Love of Money

1. Caux, situated above the Lake of Geneva in Switzerland, houses the international conference centre of Moral Re-Armament. This centre was acquired in 1946 thanks to the sacrificial giving of 70 Swiss families. International conferences have been held in Caux every summer since its opening.

2. *Tocqueville's America - The Great Quotations*, ed. Frederick Kershner, Jr, (Ohio University Press, 1983) p 19, taken from Alexis de Tocqueville, *Democracy in America* translated by Henry Reeve, revised by Francis Bowen, (Alfred A Knopf, New York 1973).

3. Countess Marion Dönhoff in *Die Zeit*, 22.9.89.

4. John Stuart Mill, (1806-1873) *On Liberty*, published 1859, (Penguin Books 1985) pp 130 and 187.

5. Flora Lewis in *International Herald Tribune*, 17.4.89.

Chapter 10, The Pervasiveness of Permissiveness

1. John Wesley (1703-1791) and his brother Charles (1707-1788) who were responsible for the Methodist Revival.

2. William Wilberforce (1759-1833), English politician, inspired by John Wesley, who led the campaign against slavery and for the 'reformation of manners', with his friends who lived close to him in Clapham.

3. Quakers, a popular name for the Society of Friends, based on seeking God through silence, founded in the middle of the seventeenth century by George Fox. Several of his followers engaged effectively in social reform; for example Elizabeth Fry (1780-1845) who did more than any other person for the reform of the prisons.

4. John Henry Newman (1801-1890), one of the leaders in a spiritual revival in the catholic tradition of the Anglican Church through the Oxford Movement. In 1845 he was received into the Roman Catholic Church (see *Apologia Pro Vita Sua*) and later became Cardinal.
Notes 1-4 see also G M Trevelyan, *English Social History* (Longmans, Green and Co., London 1944) pp 494-5.

5. Paul Johnson *A History of the Modern World* (Weidenfeld Paperbacks 1984) p 13.

Chapter 11, The Struggle for Values

1. *St Matthew's Gospel*, chapters 5, 6, and 7.

2. *St Matthew's Gospel*, chapter 5, vs 27 and 28.

3. *St Mark's Gospel*, chapter 12, vs 28-32. See also *St John's Gospel*, chapter 13, v 34.

4. *St Matthew's Gospel*, chapter 5 v 8.

Chapter 12, The Desire for Gratification

1. Dr Adu-Sarkodie, in speech to 'Creators of Peace' conference, February 1992, Harare, Zimbabwe.
2. *The Observer* 24.11.91
3. *For A Change* magazine, 'Ear to the Ground', February-March 1992.
4. Bryan Appleyard in *The Sunday Times* 1.12.91

Chapter 13, The Bondage of Addiction

1. *National Geographic*, February 1992, article by Boyd Gibbons, *Alcohol, The Legal Drug*.
2. *British Medical Journal*, editorial, 22.2.92 and 9.5.92.
3. *British Medical Journal*, editorial, 9.5.92.
4. *British Medical Journal*, editorial, 9.5.92.
5. *The Sunday Times*, 16.2.92.

Chapter 14, Focus on the Family

1. The Ten Commandments, *Exodus* chapter 20.
2. See Annejet Campbell, *Listen for a Change*, (Grosvenor Books, 1986).
3. *British Medical Journal* editorial, 22.2.92.

Chapter 15, Can we be Free of our Reactions?

1. Dieter E Zimmer, *Das sogenannte Unbewusste*, (*Zeitmagazin* 8.11.85).
2. Max Frisch, *Montauk* translated by Geoffrey Skelton (Harcourt Brace Jovanovich 1976) pp 109 and 110.

Chapter 17, The Antidote to Bitterness

1. *For A Change* magazine, told in full by Michael Smith, May 1991

2. Irina Ratushinskaya *Poet against the lie* (Grosvenor Books, 1991) p 10, a talk at the Westminster Theatre, London, 23.4.91. See also *Grey is the Colour of Hope*, translated by Alyona Kojevnikov, (Sceptre, 1989).

3. Loring Swaim, *Arthritis, Medicine and the Spiritual Laws* (Blandford Press 1963).

4. See also *For A Change* magazine, April 1991, article by John Lester, *Ireland and the English Question*.

Chapter 18, Freedom and 'the Other'

1. Günter Grass in *Frankfurter Allgemeine Zeitung*, 13.6.89.

2. See also Hans Küng, *Global Responsibility: in search of a new world ethic* (SCM Press, 1991).

Chapter 19, Freedom and Power

1. Brian Crozier, *The Masters of Power* (Eyre & Spottiswoode, London 1969) p 9.

2. Father Jozef Tischner, *The Spirit of Solidarity*, (Harper & Row, San Francisco, 1984) pp 58-59.

3. Romano Guardini, *Die Macht* (Werkbund Verlag, Wurzburg 1952), p 25.

4. Andrei Sakharov, *Decree on Power* (*Frankfurter Allgemeine Zeitung*, 14.6.89).

5. *Christian Graf von Krockow, Die Deutschen in ihrem Jahrhundert – 1890-1990* (Rowohlt Verlag, Reinbek 1990) p 291.

6. James Madison, *The Federalist*, Nr 51, 344.

7. Guardini, op. cit., p 46.

Chapter 20, The Paradox of Love

1. *St John's Gospel* chapter 3, v 16.

2. *St Luke's Gospel* chapter 22, v 42 (New International Version).

3. *Acts of the Apostles*, chapter 9.

4. *The Journal of John Wesley* vol 1, Standard Edition (Epworth Press, 1938) pp 475-6.

5. Garth Lean, *Frank Buchman: a Life* (Constable 1985) p 31.

6. See *The Little Flowers of St Francis*, translated by E M Blaiklock and A C Keys, (Hodder & Stoughton Christian Classics, 1985).

7. For St Clare see Elizabeth Goudge *St Francis of Assisi* (Hodder & Stoughton, 1961).

8. Thérèse of Lisieux, *Autobiography of a Saint*, (Collins, Fount Paperbacks 1977) originally *The Story of a Soul*, translated by Ronald Knox, 1958.

9. *Ephesians* chapter 3 v 1 and *Philemon*, v 1.

10. The coming of the Holy Spirit foretold by Jesus, *St John's Gospel*, chapter 16, v 13. The experience of Pentecost, *Acts of Apostles* chapter 2. Also *Romans* chapter 5 v 5.

11. R C Mowat, *Decline and Renewal, Europe Ancient and Modern* (New Cherwell Press, Oxford 1991) p 114.

Chapter 21, Free to Care

1. Vincent Ferrer Blehl, SJ, *A Newman Prayer Book* p 4, (Newman Secretariat, Birmingham 1990).

2. John R Mott, *The Evangelisation of the World in this Generation* (London 1901).

3. Henry Drummond, (1851-1897), natural scientist, university professor, writer and evangelist, *The Greatest Thing in the World and twenty-one other Addresses* (Collins 1972) p 294: 'Obedience is the organ of spiritual knowledge. As the eye is the organ of physical sight; the mind of intellectual sight; so the organ of spiritual vision is this strange power, obedience.'